Surviving the Loss
of a
Loved One

by
Anthony M. Coniaris

Revised and Expanded
Fourth Printing

Light & Life Publishing Company
Minneapolis, Minnesota
www.light-n-life.com

Dedicated to Presbytera Mary Coniaris + July 23, 1991

The Greek Experience
Books, Music, Video, Art
www.GreeceInPrint.com
262 Rivervale Rd, River Vale, N.J. 07675
Tel 201-664-3494 Email info@GreeceInPrint.com

Light & Life Publishing Company
Minneapolis, MN
www.light-n-life.com

Copyright © 1992
Light & Life Publishing Company

4th Printing © 2017

Various Bible versions used according to preference of the author.

ISBN No. 0-937032-89-1

Table of Contents

Coping with Grief 1
A Description of Grief 3
A State of Shock (Part 1) 5
A State of Shock (Part 2) 7
Grief Work 9
An Amputation 11
Grief Wants to be Heard 13
Grief Leads to Growth 15
Say Goodbye (Part 1) 17
Say Goodbye (Part 2) 19
Let God Love You 20
Why Me? 21
The Atmosphere of Healing (Part 1) 23
The Atmosphere of Healing (Part 2) 25
The Pain of Anniversaries 27
Learn to Say Thanks 29
A Word About Self-pity 31
Don't Rush into a New Relationship 33
Will It Ever End? 35
Change Places 37
One Actress' Grief 39
David's Grief 41
Common Misconceptions (Part 1) 43
Common Misconceptions (Part 2) 45
Avoid Mediums 47
How to Deal with Guilt 49
The Dash 51

Who's Perfect? 53
Offload Your Grief onto God 55
Turn Your Loved One over to God 57
Leave Your Grief with Him 59
What Hurts Me? 61
God Uses Our Brokenness 63
Plastic Garbage Bags 64
Broken to be More Beautiful 65
Cultivate the Awareness of God's Presence 67
My First Christmas Without David 69
Living in the Future 71
God Gives Grace for Each Day 73
Do Something in Memory of Your Loved One 75
Confessions of an Oncology Nurse 77
You Are Married to Your Friends 78
A Welcoming Committee in Heaven 79
"We" Experiences in Life 81
The Icon of the Falling Asleep of the Theotokos 82
Easing the Pain of Loss 83
If No Tears, The Body Will Weep 85
Tears: A Gift of God 87
Live a Connected Life 89
Come, Let Us Bestow the Final Kiss 90
Enveloped by God's Presence .91
Spread it Out Before the Lord .93
The Serenity of Death 95
Mary Magdalene's Tears 97
Men Fare Worse than Women .99
Word Therapy. 100
Face the Storm 101

A Flicker of Light 102
Two Empty Tombs 103
Replace "If Only" with "In Spite Of" 105
Grief is Like a Thunderstorm 107
Angels Meet Us at Death 109
Angels Will be There to Help Us 111
Present with Us in Every Liturgy 113
The Joy of Heaven 115
Not an End but a Beginning 117
Goodbye for Now, Dear 119
The Difference Between Grieving and Mourning 122
Sleep (or Lack Thereof) 124
Exercise 126
Finding Meaning in Grief 127
What We Had Was a Gift 129
Refusing to Face Reality 131
Our Church Calendar 133
Focus on Ourselves 135
Why Do We Pray for the Dead? (Part 1) 137
Why Do We Pray for the Dead? (Part 2) 139
What Can We Expect of our Prayers for the Dead? 141
A Meaningful Custom 143
Love Never Forgets 145
Dealing with Anger 147
A Parade of Memories 149
Valley of Dry Bones (Ezekiel 37) 151

Coping with Grief

Ben Franklin said once, "Nothing is certain but death and taxes." I would like to change Franklin's words to read, "Nothing is certain but grief and taxes." Since even taxes are a big grief, we could say that the only certain thing in life is grief.

I say grief because it is not just the death of a loved one that brings grief. Frequently death is an easier grief to go through than other losses like divorce or a debilitating disease. Grief consists of the emotions we experience when we lose anything or anyone we care about deeply. An amputee who loses an arm or a leg experiences grief. When you load all your belongings in a van and kiss your family and friends goodbye, grief travels with you. In youth, a boy may grieve when a romance breaks up. Grief may touch a worker when he retires, or parents when their daughter goes to college or a son goes off to the army. Some of these are losses that do not go away, but remain ever present with you and may be even more difficult to deal with than death.

All of us, therefore, will know grief. Perhaps some of you are grieving now. Everywhere we look are scores of people suffering grief. Sometimes their grief is as evident as a tear. At other times grief hides behind activity and made-up smiles. We are – most of us – in the company of the walking wounded.

How then can we handle grief? How can we survive life's losses? How can we comfort those who mourn around us? Come, travel through this book for some answers.

I will not leave you desolate; I will come to you... because I live, you will live also.

~ John 14:18

Let not your hearts be troubled; believe in God, believe also in me. In my Father's house are many rooms: if it were not so, would I have told you that I go to prepare a place for you? And when I go and prepare a place for you, I will come again and will take you to myself, that where I am you may be also.

~ John 14:1-3

Come to me, all who labor and are heavy laden, and I will give you rest. Take my yoke upon you, and learn from me; for I am gentle and lowly in heart, and you will find rest for your souls. For my yoke is easy, and my burden is light.

~ Matthew 11:28-30

In grieving, we embark on a journey through our own soul's seasons...
fall...
  winter...
    then, spring...
      finally, summer once more...
... a journey through death and loss into renewal and life

~ A.R. Bozarth

A Description of Grief

St. Paul speaks of death as having a sting. Others describe death as a knockout blow in the pit of one's stomach. C. S. Lewis described his grief when he lost his wife as follows: "No one told me that grief felt so like fear. I am not afraid, but the sensation is like being afraid. The same fluttering in the stomach, the same restlessness, the yawning. I keep on swallowing. At times I feel like being mildly drunk. There is a sort of invisible blanket between the world and me. I find it hard to take in what anyone says. Or perhaps, hard to want to take it in. It is so uninteresting. Yet I want others to be about me. I dread the moments when the house is empty…"

One widow described her grief as follows: "A truth I learned early in life is that you are never prepared for the death of a loved one. You may sit at the bedside of a loved one or friend, even pray that he or she can be released from this life of suffering, but when that moment arrives, you are not prepared. The total and final loss is overwhelming, almost frightening. This is when we must know that the divine inner strength is there if we but remember that we are not alone ever. If His eye is on the sparrow, it is certainly on you and me."

Author Edgar Jackson poignantly describes grief:

Grief is a young widow trying to raise her three children, alone.

Grief is the man so filled with shocked uncertainty and confusion that he strikes out at the nearest person.

Grief is a mother walking daily to a nearby cemetery to stand quietly and alone for a few minutes before going about the tasks of her day. She knows that part of her is in the cemetery, just as part of her is in her daily work.

Grief is the silent, knifelike terror and sadness that comes a hundred times a day, when you start to speak to someone who is no longer there.

Grief is the emptiness that comes when you eat alone after eating with another for many years.

Grief is teaching yourself to go to bed without saying good night to the one who has died.

Grief is the helpless wishing that things were different when you know they are not and never will be again.

Grief is a whole cluster of adjustments, apprehensions, and uncertainties that strike life in its forward progress and make it difficult to redirect the energies of life.

A State of Shock (Part 1)

One of the first things that happens when one experiences a great loss is that one goes into a state of shock in which one simply can't believe it's true. This is a protective reaction of great value that God gives us, because it gives a person time to muster his inner resources in order to face the full significance of the loss. This feeling helps create insulation from the reality of the death until you are more able to tolerate what you don't want to believe. This is why we should not try to comfort our friends in the first shock of bereavement. What they need more than anything else during this initial period of shock is our presence and our touch – much more than words.

Anne Morrow Lindbergh described the state of shock as follows: "The first days of grief are not the worst. The immediate reaction is usually shock and numbing disbelief. One has undergone an amputation. After shock comes acute early grief. One still feels the lost limb down to the nerve endings."

Be gracious to me, O Lord, for I am languishing;
O Lord, heal me, for my bones are troubled…
I am weary with my moaning; every night I flood my bed with tears; I drench my couch with weeping…
The Lord has heard my supplication; the Lord accepts my prayer.

~ Psalm 6:2, 6, 9

If Jesus was given a crown of thorns, His followers cannot expect a bed of roses.

~ *Anonymous*

Don't be surprised, dear friends, at the painful trials you are suffering, as though something strange were happening to you. But rejoice that you participate in Christ's suffering, so that you may be overjoyed when His glory is revealed.

~ *1 Peter 4:12-13*

I have never thought that Christians would be free of suffering. For our Lord suffered. And I have come to believe that He suffered, not to save us from suffering, but to teach us how to bear suffering.

~ *Alan Paton*

God Has Promised

God could have kept Daniel out of the lion's den. He could have kept Paul and Silas out of jail. He could have kept the three Hebrew children out of the fiery furnace. But God has never promised to keep us out of hard places. What He has promised is to go with us through every hard place, and to bring us through victoriously!

A State of Shock (Part 2)

A widow described her initial state of shock as follows:

My husband died in 1973. We were in Scottsdale, Arizona, alone in our apartment. When his death came, I became a robot. I was completely organized in my thoughts and actions. I did every thing as I normally would like a robot. I wanted to spare my family. I stayed in a state of shock for about two weeks. I went into Lund's for groceries one day and suddenly I realized I was buying for one person and I completely fell apart. I left my basket in the aisle and fled for home. That was a very necessary point in my grief. I had not cried hard before that. Here is where you begin to pick up the pieces. You suddenly know you are alone. So how do you cope? The three F's are important: Faith, Family and Friends.

A person who lost his brother to cancer said, "I can remember shouting loudly... once the numbness wore off, and I was somewhere in between feeling thankful that my brother didn't have to suffer anymore, and missing him so much that it hurt my stomach. 'You got me through the roughest part, Lord! Now please get me through the remembering'." He was describing the pain of working through one's grief.

The disciples woke him and said to him, "Teacher, don't you care if we drown?" He got up, rebuked the wind and said to the waves, "Quiet! Be still!" Then the wind died down and it was completely calm. [Jesus] said to his disciples, "Why are you so afraid? Do you still have no faith?" They were terrified and asked each other, "Who is this? Even the wind and the waves obey him!"

~ Mark 4:38-41

This is Jesus Christ, the mighty Son of the living God. This is the One who promises rest for the weary and calls us to trust him like little children. No matter what storm is frightening you right now, it is not greater than the power of Jesus.

One day Dr. Alfred Russell Wallace, a famous British naturalist, came upon a butterfly just as it was struggling to force its way through the narrow neck of its cocoon. It seemed a pity that the frail creature should go through such an ordeal, so the great scientist gently slit the cocoon with his pocket knife, taking care not to injure the emerging butterfly. Presently it was free. But the gorgeous tints of the butterfly never flashed in the sunlight nor balanced delicately on a flower. Why? Because there had been no struggle, which is the Creator's way of sending the vital fluid through the new body and into the delicate traceries of the unfolding wings of a butterfly. Only through the strength gained through struggle, faith put to the test and proven, can we climb the steep ascent to heaven.

Grief Work

One of the outstanding persons in the field of grief therapy is Dr. Erich Lindemann, former professor of psychiatry at Harvard. He concluded that a grief sufferer must work through his or her grief step by step in order to experience what he calls the "good grief." Lindemann called this process "grief work." Grief work involves dealing with complex emotions all related to the crisis of bereavement. We grieve because of self-pity ("What will become of me now that he is gone?"). We grieve because of anger ("After all I've done for her during her illness, how could she leave me?"). We grieve because of guilt ("If I had only known, I would have..."). All these emotions are important and permissible. These feelings, even some very negative ones, must be accepted, expressed and worked through before healing can begin. This is part of the work of grief.

In grief work the sufferer must be set free from "bondage to the deceased," says Dr. Lindemann, so that he or she can live an independent life with "an image of the deceased," which means to be able to live constructively and peacefully with the memories, the hurts, the joys, and the sorrows of the past. Dr. Lindemann believed mourners are never healed until they have worked through their grief. And believe me it is work that is both hard and painful. No one else can do it for us. There are no substitutes in the game of life as there are in games like baseball. In life we have to stay in the lineup and face the music, but always with God's help.

St. Paul thanked God for his "thorn in the flesh," a chronic ailment that troubled him constantly. He discovered that "God's power is made perfect in weakness" (2 Cor. 12:9). As long as he was weak, he kept clinging to his source of power in Christ. Thus it was that he thanked God for the strength that he found through his weakness.

In the tradition of St. Paul, another Christian thanked God for his thorn:

> *My God, I have never thanked Thee for my thorn. I have thanked Thee a thousand times for my roses, but not once for my thorn. I have been looking forward to a world where I should get compensation for my crosses, but I have never thought of my cross as itself a present glory. Thou, Divine Love, whose human path has been perfected through sufferings, teach me the value of my thorn... and I shall be able to say, "It was good for me that I have been afflicted".*

The Son of God suffered unto death not that we might be exempt from suffering but that our suffering might be like His.

~ Bishop Kallistos Ware

The more the sufferings of Christ abound in us, the greater will our consolation in Christ become.

~ St. Isaac the Syrian

An Amputation

In the death of a loved one, we are dealing with an amputation. We Americans tend to be impatient with persons who grieve. "Why doesn't he snap out of it?" we say. But it's an amputation. Every touch of medicine is valued, every band-aid, but we're still dealing with an amputation.

A person spoke thoughtfully of how bitter a person she would be were it not for her Christian faith. It was the anniversary of the death of her adorable young daughter 36 years ago, and she was still an amputee. Peacefully, now, but an amputee.

God Does Not Waste Anything

A friend of mine found the following message her recently deceased mother had placed in a scrapbook:

> *God will not waste anything if we give Him a chance to redeem it. He is not only a Redeemer of our sins, but He is a Redeemer of our circumstances as well. He will not waste a single problem, a single heartache, a single tear, a single grief. Our God is a Redeemer God, and He stands minute by minute before us, inviting us to let Him have the sorrow, to let Him have the pain, the grief, to let Him have the disappointment and to trust Him to make something useful, something creative of every tragedy that darkens our lives.*

Now is my soul troubled. And what should I say — "Father, save me from this hour"? No, it is for this reason that I have come to this hour.

~ John 12:27

The Lord your God is with you. He is mighty to save. He will take great delight in you; He will quiet you with His love; He will rejoice over you with singing.

~ Zephaniah 3:17

I haven't lost my wife because I know where she is. You haven't lost anything when you know where it is. Death can hide but it cannot divide.

~ V. Havner

H. was a splendid thing; a soul straight, bright, and tempered like a sword. But not a perfected saint. A sinful woman married to a sinful man; two of God's patients, not yet cured. I know there are not only tears to be dried but stains to be scoured. The sword will be made even brighter.

~ C. S. Lewis

Grief Wants to be Heard

If healing is to come, grief needs to be heard. Memories need to be examined, lingered over and discussed. Anton Chekhov depicts this brilliantly in his classic short story *The Lament*. When Iona Potapov's son has died, and no one will listen to her grief, she finally, in desperation, tries to get relief by telling the story of her grief to her horse.

To be resolved, grief must be brought into the open. It must be relived and shared both verbally and emotionally. If we do not open a wound to the air, it is harder to heal. There is consolation in finding someone to talk to. The listener does not have to offer advice or cite similar experiences he or she may have suffered. The one who grieves is the one who needs to talk. He or she is frustrated if the listener seeks to avoid discussing the cause of the grief.

Many people hesitate to visit a bereaved person because they don't know what to say. The bereaved person doesn't want you to say anything. He wants to hold your hand and talk about his grief. So, ask questions and let him or her do the talking. Shakespeare said it well, "Give sorrow words. The grief that does not speak whispers the o'er fraught heart and bids it break."

A grief-stricken woman tells of the comfort she received from a friend: "I think of the woman in my community who comforted me when I received the phone call telling of my young brother's death. She came up and put her arm around my shoulders and held me as I cried. What a wonderful comfort I felt at that moment. I was not alone in my pain; I knew she cared; I knew she was there feeling the pain with me."

Still, when we honestly ask ourselves which persons in our lives mean the most to us, we often find that it is those who, instead of giving much advice, solutions, or cures, have chosen rather to share our pain and touch our wounds with a gentle and tender hand. The friend who can be silent with us in a moment of despair or confusion, who can stay with us in an hour of grief and bereavement, who can tolerate not-knowing, not-curing, not-healing and face with us the reality of our powerlessness, that is the friend who cares.

~ Father Henri Nouwen

I would always remind members of our church grief support and growth group, "If you have no place to cry, come here and we'll cry with you, but don't expect us to offer you a Kleenex, because that act means stop crying, and we do not want you to stop crying.

~ A.C.

Grief Leads to Growth

One person has described the grief process as a "journey" in which one leaves home for a new land, and returns as an "enlarged self." Everyone suffers in life. But the important thing is not what happens to us, but how we respond to what happens to us. If suffering is met with faith, it can lead to spiritual growth. We must bear the pain and sorrow of the cross before we can experience the joy of the resurrection. We are never altogether the same after we have passed through grief as we were before. It has a humanizing and fertilizing influence on us. Indeed, they are poor who have never suffered and have none of sorrow's marks upon them.

Paula D'Arcy expressed this well in her book *When Your Friend is Grieving*:

> *Grief has been my great teacher. Its primary gifts have been an abiding faith in God, an awareness that the present moments of life matter deeply, and a knowing that my everyday choices are powerful. Through them, I either affirm life, or I do not.*
>
> *Grief has taught me to cling to nothing – except my hope in God; to reject nothing, but to learn from everything. Through death, we all will eventually lose the presence of those whom we love. But we won't lose love. The very grief that wounded me has made me rich. And if you love someone through the grieving process, the deep lessons of grief are also yours.*[1]

---

1 Harold Shaw Publishers. Wheaton, IL, ©1990

Christ is risen! He is risen indeed and the sting of death has been taken away. Although death is still active among us, it does not reign any more. The victory of the risen Christ, not yet fully disclosed, will be fully actualized at the General Resurrection of the dead when Jesus shall return in glory.

Christ is risen! And "He has delivered us from the dominion of darkness and transferred us to the kingdom of His beloved Son, in Whom we have redemption, the forgiveness of sins" (Col. 1:13). "Let no one mourn his transgressions, for pardon has dawned from the tomb" (Chrysostom).

Christ is risen! And because of it we do not disappear into nothingness when we die. "Father, into Your hands I commit my spirit," prayed Jesus before He died. We die and pass on to God, to His light, His love, His power, His kingdom. "Let no one fear death, for the Savior's death has set us free! He that was taken by death has annihilated death" (Chrysostom).

Death be not proud, though some have called thee
Mighty and dreadful, for, thou art not so...
One short sleep past, we wake eternally.
And death shall be no more.
Death thou shalt die.

~ John Donne

Say Goodbye (Part 1)

One other task we need to complete in our grief work is to say goodbye to a relationship that does not exist any more. We do not say goodbye to the person, to the memories, or to the hopes of future reunion. But we must say goodbye to the relationship as it was and can be no longer.

A certain person tells of going to the cemetery one day soon after the funeral, standing over the grave, and saying to her mom, "Goodbye, mom. I love you." As she left the cemetery, no longer tense, she said, "How I needed to say that goodbye. Now I can begin to let go and move on."

We need to say goodbye to the old before we can move on to the new. No matter how much it hurts, we must say that goodbye. Not saying goodbye can leave one wounded and in pain all of one's life. Despite this, let us remember that Christians never say goodbye for the last time. It is only a temporary goodbye. And let's remember that goodbye is a contraction of "God be with you."

A grieving person once said, "I don't want to die, but it hurts too much to live."

The Resurrection icon shows Christ – not standing alone – but raising, lifting, Adam and Eve out of the depths through the broken doors of Hades. He frees patriarch, prophet and king. But, at the same time, He frees us. He sets at liberty our own life. That hand that reaches out to grasp the hand of Adam reaches out to embrace Adam's descendants as well. For we, too, are bound by death. We, too, are held captive by the power of sin. We, too, have "died" and been cast into the farthest reaches of the abyss. Yet the Risen Savior comes to us as to lost sheep, descending in His compassionate love to seek us out in the darkness and to raise us up with Himself. Like the Hound of Heaven, He pursues us down the byways. If we make our bed in hell, He is there, ever present, ever reaching out to draw us with Him into the glory of the resurrected life. From anxiety in the face of death, He raises us to an unshakeable hope in the resurrected life. From fear of the future, He raises us to an undiminished joy. From loneliness and separation. He raises us to friendship with God, nay, to partakers of His divine glory.

One flesh. Or, if you prefer, one ship. The starboard engine has gone. I, the port engine, must chug along somehow till we make harbor. Or rather, till the journey ends.

~ *C.S. Lewis*

Say Goodbye (Part 2)

We must always look at our suffering through the lens of our faith in the resurrection of Jesus. We must look at the hello that stands behind our goodbyes. We say goodbye to a loved one at the airport. He or she disappears over the horizon but we know that soon there will be a beautiful hello. We must stand strong in the resurrection, believing that there is something beyond death; there is something beyond pain and hurt and heartache. Here is where our strength and hope lie. This is the power of the resurrection at work in us:

> *Do not grieve as those who have no hope. We believe that Jesus died and rose again, and that it will be the same for those who have died in Jesus: God will bring them with Him (1 Thess. 4:13-14).*

Goodbyes will always be with us, but so will the hellos. Because of our faith in the resurrection of our Lord, we know that farewells and goodbyes are not forever because we live with faith in the eternal hello. St. Paul expressed it well when he wrote, "I think that what we suffer in this life (the goodbyes) can never be compared to the glory (the hellos) as yet unrevealed which is waiting for us" (Rom. 8:18).

A Christian martyr was asked once, "Why are you not afraid of death?" He replied, "Because I have already died." What he meant was, "I have already said goodbye to sin and to the things of this world. I am ready to hear the eternal hello from Jesus when He will say to me, 'Well done, good and faithful servant... Come enter into the joy of your Master. You have been faithful over little. I will set you over much... inherit the kingdom prepared for you from the foundation of the world'" (Matt. 25:23,34).

Let God Love You

A friend came in one day to visit a retired bishop who was in a home for terminal cancer patients. "How are you doing?" he asked. The bishop replied, "I'm just sitting here letting God love me."

Why not do the same as you grieve? Just sit there in God's presence and let God love you as you grieve. Is He not closer to you than the air you breathe? And who loves you more than God? And do you not belong to Him by right of creation as well as by right of redemption? Let God love you. Let God grieve with you. "Cast all your cares upon Him, for He cares for you" (1 Pet. 5:7).

We were made not primarily that we may love God (though we were made for that too) but that God may love us, that we may become objects in which the Divine love may rest "well pleased."

~ *C.S. Lewis*

Why Me?

People often ask when something bad happens to them, "Why me?" This question certainly expresses the anguish of one's soul when a loved one dies. Yet we need to ask the same question when confronted with all the blessings we receive from the Lord Jesus. If we believe in "the cross, the tomb, the resurrection on the third day, the ascension into heaven, the enthronement at the right hand of the Father and the second glorious coming," as we pray in the liturgy, then by all means let us ask, "Why me?"

The eternal Son of God – Jesus – took on flesh to become a Brother and Friend and Savior for me. Why me? Jesus loves me. Why me? Jesus suffered and died on the cross for me. Why me? Jesus descended into hell and destroyed forever the gates of Hades for me. Why me? Jesus walks beside me and lives inside me. Why me? Jesus ascended into heaven with His human nature to raise me to heaven. Why me? Jesus wants me to be in heaven with Him to behold His glory forever. Why me? Jesus wants me to be a "partaker of divine nature" and to achieve union with Him. Why me? God the Father sends the Holy Spirit to abide in me, making me a Temple of the Holy Spirit. Why me? Jesus will come again to give me "the life of the ages to come." Why me?

In this world we all need to face Job's question, "Shall we accept good from God and not trouble?" But in the world to come, where God will be all in all, and where we will forever enjoy God and reign with Him, our grateful and most awesome question will forever be, "Why me?"

No satisfying understanding of suffering can be achieved if one considers only this life and this world which we know. The context of an endless, eternal life must be in the background of an exploration of suffering.

~ John Powell

A God Who loved us so much as to die for us was not going to be frustrated by death. The power of death came under His control. So now we confess with St. Paul: "None of us lives to himself, and none of us dies to himself. If we live, we live to the Lord, and if we die, we die to the Lord; so, then, whether we live or whether we die, we are the Lord's" *(Rom. 14:7-8).*

...do not grieve like those who have no hope. We believe that Jesus died and rose again, and that it will be the same for those who have died in Jesus: God will bring them with Him.

~ 1 Thess. 4:13-14

When I lay these questions before God I get no answer. But a rather special sort of "no answer." It is not the locked door. It is more like a silent, certainly not uncompassionate, gaze. As though He shook His head not in refusal but waiving the question. Like, "Peace, child, you don't understand."

~ C.S. Lewis

The Atmosphere of Healing (Part 1)

In an article written following the death of his wife in 1989, Fr. Joseph Allen said, "I know now that it was precisely a certain atmosphere which led to (my) healing: that atmosphere was God's community, celebrated in the Eucharist, practiced in the everyday life of the parish, enlivened in the communion of love, not really of 'parishioners,' but of veritable brothers and sisters in the Lord – these are the elements of care through which God's grace has flowed into my life, and thus, healed me."

The healing atmosphere of grief includes the three F's: faith, family and friends. Faith includes the Church which is God's family, the fellowship of our caring brothers and sisters in Christ who bear one another's burdens. A parish grief support group is an excellent expression of this healing outreach of God's people to the bereaved.

The healing atmosphere of faith includes daily prayer. Dr. Paul Tournier wrote about prayer: "In the past I have often skipped my daily meditation, but since my wife's death, I have not missed a single day – as if my rendezvous with God was a rendezvous with her."

The healing atmosphere of grief includes God's Word, the Holy Bible and its many beautiful promises.

Whosoever believes in me shall never die.

~ John 11:26

Beloved, we are God's children now; it does not yet appear what we shall be, but we know that when He appears we shall be like Him, for we shall see Him as He is.

~ 1 John 3:2

May the God of hope fill you with all joy and peace in believing, so that by the power of the Holy Spirit you may abound in hope.

~ Romans 15:13

I go to prepare a place for you, I will come again and receive you unto myself; that where I am, there you may be also.

~ John 14:3

I am the resurrection and the life; whoever believes in Me, though he were dead, yet shall he live, and whoever lives and believes in Me shall never die.

~ John 11:25-26

For if we have been united with Him in a death like His, we shall certainly be united with Him in a resurrection like His... But if we have died with Christ, we believe we shall also live with Him.

~ Romans 6:5,8

Will you not now after Life has descended to you, will you not ascend to it and live?

~ St. Augustine

Christ is risen! And because of it, "The angels rejoice! Life reigns in freedom! And there is none left dead in the tomb!"

~ St. John Chrysostom

The Atmosphere of Healing (Part 2)

In addition to faith, the Church, prayer and the promises of God, the healing atmosphere of grief includes family. When moments of depression begin to descend upon me, I have been helped either by spending time with my son's family at their lake cabin, or by walking around a nearby lake with my married daughter, talking and even crying as we walked. The combination of the physical exercise of walking combined with expressing grief by talking and crying has been most healing. How true the proverb, "He who goes too far alone goes mad."

The healing atmosphere of grief includes, in addition to family, *friends*. One person writes, "Let me tell you what the doctor who attended my wife did for me as I stood dazed and lost at the foot of her bed, knowing not only that the 37 years we had had together were over, but feeling also that all meaning had gone from life forever. He took my arm and held it for a moment. And then he said in a matter-of-fact voice: 'You'll see her again.' That was all. But it was all I needed to hear."

Thank God for the healing atmosphere of faith, the Church, prayer, God's word, family and friends. May those of us who are bereaved bask in their healing presence each day.

I like the words of St. Paul, "Praised be... the God of all comfort, who comforts us in all our troubles, so that we can comfort those in any trouble with the comfort we ourselves have received from God" (2 Cor. 1:3-4). We are comforted by God, says St. Paul, that we may pass on this comfort to others.

My grace is sufficient for you, for my power is made perfect in weakness.

~ *2 Corinthians 12:9*

Unless a grain of wheat falls into the earth and dies, it remains alone; but if it dies, it bears much fruit... If any one serves me, he must follow me; and where I am, there shall my servant be also.

~ *John 12:24,26*

That I may know Him and the power of His resurrection, and may share in His sufferings, becoming like Him in His death.

~ *Philippians 3:10*

We do not honor the dead by dying with them, so "wait for the Lord; be strong and take heart and wait for the Lord."

~ *Psalm 31:24*

The God Who holds the sea in the hollow of His hand, Who swings the ponderous earth in its orbit, Who marshals stars and guides planets, is the very God Who says, "If you ask, I will do it."

~ *J.H. McConkey*

The Pain of Anniversaries

Anniversaries will always be painful for those who grieve. That is why the Church in her wisdom has given us memorial services. Why not celebrate a memorial service in church on those anniversaries? What is more healing to grief than a prayer in church with your church family?

Special days are hard to take. But here again, a day is only 24 hours long. It will pass. Take God into your day. Plan ahead. Get yourself out. Make yourself do something different. Remember God's promise, "For I, the Lord, will be with you and see you through" (Jer. 1:8).

A critical time is the first anniversary of the death or the birthday of the deceased. I was helped in my own grief over my wife's death when I suddenly remembered on her birthday that the feast days of the saints that are commemorated by the Church are the days on which each of these saints died. The day of their death is their real birthday, i.e., the day of their birth into eternal life with God. I then came to realize that my wife's real birthday from now on was the day of her death. On this day it is comforting to remember our loved ones with a special memorial prayer service.

Is it Christmas? Your loved one would not want you to grieve without hope. He or she is now celebrating Christmas in heaven. Aim to enjoy this Christmas with your family and friends as though it were your very best.

Your death, O Lord, became the cause of immortality, for if You had not been placed in a tomb, paradise would not have been opened.

~ Orthodox Funeral Hymn

An author once said in a newspaper interview, "I don't think there will ever be definitive proof of life after death in the strict sense. I believe this is more a matter of faith."

This statement is foolish, misleading and completely unhistorical. The resurrection faith is firmly based on the solid resurrection fact. When Jesus appeared in the upper room to His discouraged disciples, He said, "Look at my hands and look at my side. It is I, Myself" (John 20:27).

The greatest event in recorded history is the resurrection of Jesus Christ. It has been called "history's turning point." Because He lives, we too shall live.

Did you ever know, dear, how much you took away with you when you left? You have stripped me even of my past, even of the things we never shared. I was wrong to say the stump was recovering from the pain of the amputation. I was deceived because it has so many ways to hurt me that I discover them only one by one.

~ C.S. Lewis

Learn to Say Thanks

An essential part of healing for grief is to remember to say thanks for all the blessings God gave us, all the happy memories. God gave me my spouse, my children, my grandchildren, my many friends who care and came to express their sympathy, and I need to say thank you. A young widow with two small children, who had lost her husband in a battle with leukemia, said that the first light that came in the darkness of grief was when she learned to say thank you. Thank you, for all that was and thank you, Lord, for all that is to be. Our times are in His hands. And He has prepared for those who love Him a future so unbelievably beautiful that it can only be called heaven. "He will wipe every tear from their eyes. There will be no more death or mourning or crying or pain, for the old order of things has passed away" (Rev. 21:4).

"Will the pain lessen with the years?" someone asked. The answer came, "Yes, because it gradually changes to gratitude."

There is nothing dreadful in that which delivers us from all that is to be dreaded.

~ *Tertullian*

It is for him to fear death who is not willing to go to Christ.

~ *Cyprian*

Getting over it so soon? But the words are ambiguous. To say the patient is getting over it after an operation for appendicitis is one thing; after he's had his leg off it is quite another. After that operation either the wounded stump heals or the man dies. If it heals, the fierce, continuous pain will stop. Presently he'll get back his strength and be able to stump about on his wooden leg. He has "gotten over it." But he will probably have recurrent pains in the stump all his life, and perhaps pretty bad ones; and he will always be a one-legged man. There will be hardly any moment when he forgets it. Bathing, dressing, sitting down and getting up again, even lying in bed, will all be different. His whole way of life will be changed. All sorts of pleasures and activities that he once took for granted will have to be simply written off. Duties too. At present I am learning to get about on crutches. Perhaps I shall presently be given a wooden leg. But I shall never be a biped again.

~ *C.S. Lewis*

A Word About Self-Pity

Let me say just a word here about self-pity. Grief can spawn self-pity very quickly. Often this self-pity is generated by the sincere sympathy of people around you. When they see you worried or weeping, it is natural for them to support you with sympathy. But instead of supporting you, their sympathy only feeds your self-pity. And self-pity is deadly. It weakens, fatigues and saps your life of strength.

How do you overcome self-pity? You've got to be tough on yourself. Tell yourself to grow up and stop acting like a baby. Say to yourself: "'Who do I think I am that I should be spared this heartache? The greatest people in the Bible, even the most wonderful friends of God, even Jesus Himself, suffered tragedy. Why should I think that I should be spared?" When you start feeling sorry for yourself, take a walk through a nursing home. Think of others who are suffering far more than you are – and reach out to help them. It's natural to experience self-pity once in a while, but don't wallow in it.

None of us is greater than our Master; we cannot have the crown without the cross.

Jesus never spoke of His suffering and death without speaking at the same time of His resurrection. Like Jesus, we need to learn to say about suffering, "Shall I not drink of the cup the Father has given me?"

I am not looking for death to come. I am looking for Jesus to come and take me home.

A few years ago I attended a funeral in a non-Orthodox church. To me, the ritual of burial was so poor and cold: they sang a few songs, the minister said something brief, and the coffin was taken away. It was like she was being torn away from us and there wasn't time to grieve. Now, our Orthodox prayers just rip the soul out of you. When you hear "With the saints give rest...", you can't not cry, you just drop to your knees and weep. It gives you the possibility of grieving deeply at that moment, and then you don't get crazy later on. There is a reason for everything in Orthodoxy.

~ A Parishioner

Don't Rush into a New Relationship

At my local parish, a priest addressed a group of newly single adults who were struggling with the nauseating feelings of loss and grief that come with death or divorce. He cautioned,

> *Be careful not to rush into new relationships just to fill the void in your lives. You have to learn to live with the emptiness. And when you have peace with the emptiness, then you can move on into a new relationship. But don't be afraid to be alone, even though it will feel horrible. And you may feel ugly and unloved and unlovable. Wait. Wait.*

But the waiting can be hard. Unwanted aloneness can cause agony. One night, very late, more recently than I'd like to admit, I was sitting at my small kitchen table. Alone and wrapped in my old terry cloth bathrobe, I believed my whole life had shriveled up into an endless parade of days. Having discovered a painful and unpleasant truth about a man I'd recently been dating. I'd been feeling sorry for myself. And I wanted that sorrowful emptiness filled up – at almost any cost.

In high school, my physics teacher told us that molecules will rush to fill an empty space because "nature abhors a vacuum." I, too, abhor vacuums. The desert of our weaknesses can be frightening, our emotional and spiritual emptiness starkly painful. We can choose to avoid this pain and fear, but the devil is in the avoidance. That was the wisdom of the priest who told us to "Wait. Wait." Many times my rushing to fill the vacuum has caused grief for me and for others. Never once, however, have I been disappointed in waiting for the Lord. God is in the desert. God knows what I look like in my bathrobe, all alone late at night. And never once has God suggested that the sight is pathetic. Instead, in those empty hours God says, "Talk to me. Then be still and know that I am God."

~ A Grieving Widow

So real is the resurrection of Jesus to the Orthodox Christian that every Sunday he is asked to pray in the Matins service this lovely prayer which speaks not of just believing in the resurrection but more especially of having beheld it:

Having beheld the resurrection of Christ,
Let us worship the holy Lord Jesus, the only sinless One. We venerate Thy Cross, O Christ, and we praise
and glorify Thy holy resurrection;
for Thou art our God and we know no other than Thee.
We call on Thy name. O Come all ye faithful,
Let us venerate Christ's holy resurrection!
For behold, through the cross joy has come into all the world.
Let us ever bless the Lord, praising his resurrection,
For by enduring the cross for us,
He has destroyed death by death.

Will It Ever End?

Will the grief ever end? It will. A proverb says, "Everything that grows begins small and becomes big; but grief starts big and becomes small – and disappears." Grief will not last forever; it will end. As Jesus said, "You will be sorrowful but your sorrow will turn into joy" (John 16:20). It is natural for us to grieve, but after a while we do recover. Grief comes to a successful end and is healed when we can remember clearly what we have lost, but now without the intense pain that we felt previously. As Fr. Joseph Allen says, "We are at peace with the past, and now live with the hope that is given by God's grace." We are now free again to invest ourselves in the new challenges and dreams of the future. Dr. Paul Tournier describes how he came to be at peace with his wife's death as follows:

I think that there is a certain amount of psychological overcompensation in my present activity, and in my writing so many books. All my work, in any case, could be interpreted as a "work of mourning." But I find it a sort of fellowship with (my late wife) Nelly: we did everything together, and in a way we still do. I have a strong sense of her invisible presence... There are widowers who, as it were, suspend their lives, as if life had stopped at the moment of their bereavement... whereas I live in the present and look to the future... my wife's presence is living and stimulating.

Dr. Tournier had not severed or abolished the attachment to his late wife. Rather, he turned it into a beautiful living presence that was stimulating and inspiring in his life. Gone was the grief that the image of his deceased wife conjured up; present now was a beautiful living presence that inspired him to continue his ministry of writing.

Therefore we do not lose heart. Though outwardly we are wasting away, yet inwardly we are being renewed day by day. For our light and momentary troubles are achieving for us an eternal glory that far outweighs them all. So we fix our eyes not on what is seen but on what is unseen. For what is seen is temporary, but what is unseen is eternal.

~ *2 Corinthians 4:16-18*

Some people come to the Orthodox midnight Easter liturgy every year to enjoy a "colorful ritual." But it is not a "colorful ritual" that fills us with joy on this great and holy day. It is the life-giving power of Christ's holy resurrection. It is the joy of His presence as we taste that risen presence and experience it in our hearts. So we sing endlessly that lovely hymn: "Christ is risen from the dead, by His death He has destroyed death and to those in the tombs He has bestowed life."

Pain is inevitable. Misery is optional.

Change Places

One helpful suggestion that may be of help to persons who have lost their spouse is to sleep on the spouse's side of the bed so as to avoid the pain of looking at the empty space formerly occupied by the departed loved one. One spouse confided that she would often place her departed husband's Bible or icon on his side of the bed.

Wait for the Lord

The Psalmist writes, "Wait for the Lord, be strong and take heart and wait for the Lord" (Ps. 27:14). When it's night, you can't do anything to make it daytime. You have to wait for the sun to rise. But that waiting can be positive waiting, eager waiting with a strong sense of expectation. You may be in the darkness of sorrow, you may not be able to see any rays of hope, but the sun will rise as He rose from the tomb and those who believe in Him will rise with Him. Our kind of waiting is based on the risen Christ. Thus, it is a positive, eager, expectant and joyful waiting, for "Christ has risen indeed."

Fear not, I am the first and the last, and the living one; I died, and behold I am alive forevermore, and I have the keys of Death and Hades.

~ Revelations 1:17-18

But God, Who is rich in mercy, out of the great love with which he loved us, even when we were dead through our trespasses, made us alive together with Christ (by grace you have been saved) and raised us up with Him, and made us sit with Him in the heavenly places in Christ Jesus, that in the coming ages He might show the immeasurable riches of His grace in kindness toward us in Christ Jesus.

~ Ephesians 2:4-7

Thou shall keep him in perfect peace, whose mind is stayed on Thee, because he trusts in Thee.

~ Isaiah 26:3

A cut finger
is numb before it bleeds
it bleeds before it hurts
it hurts until it begins to heal,
it forms a scab and itches until, finally
     the scab is gone and a small scar is
     where once there was a wound.
Grief is the deepest wound you have ever had.
Like a cut finger, it goes through stages and leaves a scar.

~ D. Manning

One Actress' Grief

Doris Day, an actress, went through a terrible struggle when her husband passed away. When asked how she came back to life again, she answered, "My faith really came alive! I had been reading my Bible, and had read the words of Christ for years. I recalled the promises of Christ, 'He who lives and believes in me shall never die.' It hit me with enormous force: God promised, and God promises life eternal!

"I found myself asking myself, 'Doris Day, do you believe in the Bible, and Jesus Christ? If so, stop storing it and start using it! Store food in a closet and it rots – use it and it will put muscle in our spirit.'

"It dawned on me – if I don't start applying God's promises – I'm a fool. When you are riding in an airplane and hit an air-pocket you drop, gasp, but the plane rises, comes back up. So it is when a loved one passes on, you drop, gasp, but then you feel the renewing power of God's uplifting spirit! Peace comes! And you sail on with His uplifting power under your wings!"

Stop telling God about your big problem and start telling your problem about your big God.

If you've ever stood at the grave of your dear one, you know how much it hurts to say goodbye. Even today, when you think about your loss, a lump rises in your throat, tears fill your eyes, an aching emptiness gnaws at your heart. A husband or wife, son or daughter, a dear friend – oh, how you miss them. If only you could embrace each other and talk together again! Well, the good news of our Risen Lord is that if you and your loved one were both united in your faith in Him, you will see each other again.

The time is coming, says God's word, when everyone will wake from the sleep of death, and all our grief will vanish like a bad dream. All who belong to Jesus will have a joyful reunion, never to be separated again.

David's Grief

When King David's little son was sick, he fasted and prostrated himself before the Lord, and would not be comforted. The seventh day the child died. The servants hesitated to tell David that the child was dead, fearing that he would do himself harm. To their surprise, when he heard it, David washed himself, dressed, anointed himself and sat down to eat. He told his servants, "While the child was still alive, I fasted and wept; for I said, 'Who knows whether the Lord will be gracious to me, that the child may live?' But now he is dead; why should I fast? Can I bring him back again? I shall go to him, but he will not return to me."

A Ticket to Heaven

A medical doctor told a Christian woman one day that she had inoperable cancer with only six months to live. The woman looked at the doctor and said, "Thank you, Doctor, for giving me my ticket to heaven."

The real ticket to heaven, of course, is faith in Jesus. "He who lives and believes in me shall have life everlasting."

The following words were written by a widow following the sudden death of her husband:

It took me many years in my marriage to learn that no man on this earth can satisfy the deepest longings of a woman's heart. Only God can do that. He is also the only one who can help me live with that deep hole, that deep pain, in my heart.

The hole is still there; He hasn't filled it up yet. But He has made a bridge over it. I can live with it now, and I can stand on this bridge as I reach out to others.

So you have sorrow now, but I will see you again and your hearts will rejoice, and no one will take your joy from you.

~ John 16:22

We do not fully say *yes* to life until we say *yes* to death. In Christ we can say *yes* to death because Christ is risen!

Many years ago when I was trying to make a difficult decision, I turned to God for guidance. As I prayed, I came up with the following thoughts, and I've referred to them again and again when faced with a problem:
* God is.
* God is good.
* God is good to me.
* God loves me – even more than I love myself.
* God knows what is best for me and lovingly works to make that happen.
* Since God is good and loves me and wants the best for me, I can say a wholehearted *yes* to what God calls me to be or do.

~ J.B. Everly

Common Misconceptions (Part 1)

Let us look for a moment at some common misconceptions concerning grief.

The first misconception is that "time heals everything." The truth is that time alone does not heal grief unless it is accompanied by all the factors we have talked about. Time needs to be filled with faith, prayer, family, friends and the honest acceptance and expression of our emotions. One authority on grief wrote, "The simple passage of time alone does not heal wounds – either physical or emotional. A healthy environment helps the process. Time alone will not heal, but what one does with time can. The key criterion for a healing environment is an attitude of acceptance and openness to human feelings and pain."

Another misconception of grief-stricken thinking is, "I'll never get over this." False! You will never be the same person because of what has happened – but the hurt will heal some day. "...weeping may remain for a night, but joy comes in the morning" (Ps. 30:5).

When Jesus arrived at Lazarus' tomb in John 11, the Greek verb that is used to describe His reaction is *enebrimisato*, which refers literally to the snort of a warhorse, or for us humans, a huge outburst of anger. Thus, at Lazarus' tomb, Jesus is outraged by death, furious about the devastation it brings. The additional Greek verb used is *etaraxen eauton*. Placed together, the reaction we get is that Jesus "roared and was greatly vexed" by death.

There is more than cancer. There is more than suffering. There is more than sorrow. There is more than death. There is God's grace. There is God's love. There is God's power. There is God's eternal life. There is God's victory in Christ Jesus.

"Who shall separate us from the love of Christ? Shall tribulation, or distress, or persecution, or famine, or nakedness, or peril or sword?... No, in all these things we are more than conquerors through Him Who loved us. For I am sure that neither death... nor anything else in all creation will be able to separate us from the love of God in Christ Jesus our Lord" (Rom. 8:35,37-39).

If any doctor ever tells us we are terminal, may we correct him by saying, "Not terminal! Not when one is a baptized believer living in the body of Christ, the Church. Transitional, yes: terminal, no!" There is more!

The cords of death encompassed me, the torrents of perdition assailed me, the cords of Sheol entangled me, the snares of death confronted me. In my distress I called upon the Lord, to my God I cried for help. From his temple he heard my voice and my cry to him reached his ears... He bowed the heavens, and came down, thick darkness was under his feet. He rode on a cherub, and flew; he came swiftly upon the wings of the wind... He reached from on high, he took me, he drew me out of many waters.

~ Psalm 18:4-6; 9-10; 16

Common Misconceptions (Part 2)

An additional misconception of grieving persons is, "I've lost everything." How false! You have not lost your loved one. You have been separated temporarily. But, there will be a blessed reunion. You will be together again – this time eternally. Our loved ones are not lost. "Eye has not seen, nor has ear heard, nor has it ever entered into the heart of man what things God has prepared for those who love Him" (1 Cor. 2:9). Do these words sound like a "loss"?

A final misconception regarding grief was expressed by a husband who was sobbing following the death of his wife. He said, "I've been such a fool. I thought she would always be here." None of us will always be here. We're pilgrims – just passing through on our way to heaven. This should make us treasure and value the precious moments we have with our loved ones on earth. It should cause us to spend quality time with them.

One human being is missing and all of life becomes a desert.

For we know that if the earthly tent we live in is destroyed, we have a building from God, a house not made with hands, eternal in the heavens" (2 Cor. 5:1). There is more!

The Risen Christ proclaims, "Because I live, you shall live also." Life here on earth is wonderful; this is a glorious world; it is the best world we have ever seen. Only God could have made it. But this earthly life isn't anything compared to what God has prepared for those who love Him. Tennyson, for example, said, "Death is the bright side of life." Life has two sides, this side and the other side. This side, says Tennyson, is the dull side. He was right. In the end, the Christian goes not to the darkness of a tomb, but to the Lord Jesus, Who is the light of the world. There is more!

"If in this life we who are in Christ have only hope, we are of all men most to be pitied" (1 Cor. 15:19). There is more!

I was crushed... so much so that I despaired even of life, but that was to make me rely on the God who raises the dead.

~ *2 Corinthians 1:8-9*

No evil is as great as the feeling of loneliness.

~ *St. Chrysostom*

Avoid Mediums

Some people in their grief feel compelled to communicate with their departed loved ones by visiting mediums who will allegedly place them in contact with the deceased person through séances. These mediums, if they are not fake, are certainly demonic. Stay away from them. If you wish to say anything to your departed loved one, tell it to Jesus in prayer and He will see to it that your loved one gets the message.

One person would communicate with his departed wife each day through the following prayer. "Dear Jesus, please tell Mary that I love her. I miss her. She was your gift to me. Thank you for our years together."

Through prayer, Christians can remain forever connected to the deceased as love and forgiveness are passed back and forth.

Our last day is our first day; our Saturday is our Sunday; our eve is our holy day; our sunsetting is our morning; the day of our death is the first day of our eternal life. The next day after that... comes that day that shall show me to myself. Here I never saw myself but in disguises; there, then, I shall see myself, but I shall see God too... Here I have one faculty enlightened, and another left in darkness; my understanding sometimes cleared, my will at the same time perverted. There I shall be all light, no shadow upon me; my soul invested in the light of my joy, and my body in the light of glory.

~ *John Donne*

How Will Our Bodies Rise Again?

St. Augustine answered this question when he wrote,

"How will our bodies rise again? Not in the way that Lazarus was brought back to life. He was raised up only for a time, and had to die again later on. We shall not come back to life in order to go on living the same kind of earthly life and pursuing the same earthly pleasures as we did before. St. Paul makes that clear. He says our bodies will be sown in the ground as natural bodies, and raised up as spiritual bodies (I Cor. 15:44). In the risen life our bodies will be fully under the control of our glorified spirits. They will no longer be a burden to us, nor will they have any need for food, since they will never suffer again or wear out. There will be no more death, no more sickness, no more hunger or thirst, no distress or old age or weariness. Our mortal bodies will put on immortality and imperishability."

Draw near to God and He will draw near to you.

~ James 4:8

My eyes became a fountain of tears.

~ Jeremiah 9:1

The hardest lesson of all...[is] to accept what we cannot understand and still say, "God, thou art love. I build my faith on that."

~ William Barclay

How to Deal with Guilt

Guilt often sets in after the loss of a loved one. The survivors may feel guilt because they did not consult the doctor sooner, or did not choose a better hospital, or for allowing the operation, etc. A good way to overcome such guilt is to test it out with reality by asking yourself, "What did I do?" Make a list of the things you did do to help the deceased. Most often you will come to the conclusion that you did all you could have done under the circumstances.

Yet we must remember that there is such a thing as real guilt over something we may have done that was indeed wrong. Such guilt we need to take to our loving Savior in prayer and in confession. His forgiving love can remove this burden from us and grant us the peace that passes all understanding. "Come to me all you who labor and are heavy laden and I will give you rest," says Jesus (Matt. 11:28). "Though your sins are as scarlet they shall be made as white as snow" (Isa. 1:18 NKJV).

Cease dwelling on the past. Reach out to embrace the future.

No sin is so great that it can conquer the munificence of the Master. Even if one is a fornicator, or an adulterer... the power of the gift and the love of the Master are great enough to make all these sins disappear and to make the sinner shine more brightly than the rays of the sun...

And Christ Himself, addressing the whole human race, said, "Come to me, all you who labor and are burdened, and I will give you the rest..." His invitation is one of kindness. His goodness is beyond description...

And see whom He calls! Those who have spent their strength in breaking the law, those who are burdened with their sins, those who can no longer lift up their heads, those who are filled with shame, those who can no longer speak out. And why does He call them? Not to demand an accounting, nor to hold court. But why? To relieve them of their pain, to take away their heavy burden. For what could ever be a heavier burden than sin?... "I shall refresh you who are weighted down by sin," He says, "and you who are bent down as if under a burden; I shall grant you remission of your sins. Only come to Me!"

~ *St. John Chrysostom*

We can only surrender to the process. And avoid comparing our recovery with another's. We each have our own timing.

The Dash

I read of a man who stood
to speak at the funeral of his friend.
He referred to the dates on her tombstone
from the beginning... to the end.

He noted that first came the date of her birth
and spoke of the second with tears,
but he said that what mattered most of all
was the dash between those years.

For that dash represents all the time
that she spent alive on earth,
and now only those who loved her know
what that little dash is worth.

For it matters not, how much we own;
the cars, the house, the cash.
What matters is how we live and love
when we're living out the dash.

If we could just slow down enough to consider
what's true and what is real,
And always try to understand
the way other people feel.

And... be less quick to anger,
and show appreciation more,
And love the people in our lives
like we've never loved before.

If we treat each other with respect,
and more often wear a smile,
Remember that this special dash
might only last a while.

So, when your eulogy is being read
With your life's actions to rehash...
will you be pleased with what there's to say
about how you spent your dash?

~ *Author Unknown*

Take a moment to recall some of the major "dashes" in your
loved one's life. Thank God for them.

Man's Greatest Fear Abolished

"The fear of death is worse than death," wrote Robert
Fulton. This fear causes a basic anxiety in us. We know we are
going to die. In fact, we begin to die from the moment of birth.
We are mortal, helpless, totally powerless in the face of death.
Life is a journey from the helplessness of birth to the helplessness of death. In order to escape this basic insecurity man tries
to amass money and power. He loses himself in the pleasures
of life. Desperately he tries to find ways to escape the ultimate
insecurity of life, i.e., the fear of death.

What Did God Do?

What does God do in all this? Does He remain in the bil-
lowy heavens above, indifferent to the agony that afflicts man?
No! He so loved us that He did something drastic. He sent His
only Son to become one of us, to die our death in order to
destroy death by His death and resurrection. Thus, He annihilated the power of death and delivered all those who through
fear of death were subject to lifelong bondage (Heb. 2:14-15).
Baptism, by which we share in Christ's death and resurrection,
now becomes a tomb and a womb, a death and a rising again to
a new life with God – a life that knows no end (Rom. 6:4).

Who's Perfect?

Most people idealize their departed loved ones. They remember only the good things about the deceased, forgetting the unpleasant things that took place. In our love for them we almost canonize them as saints. This is not unusual. It is normal to idealize a loved one who has died.

The reality of it all is that none of us is perfect. We are all on the way to perfection. St. John Climacus spoke of "The perfect but still unfinished perfection of the perfect." We are continuously cleansed and perfected through repentance as we go through life. If the holy armor of the idealized departed one is suddenly pierced by an unhappy memory of some imperfection either on your part or the deceased's, claim God's forgiveness and remember that we are all imperfect disciples now, but by God's grace growing to become one day perfected saints in God's kingdom.

Let us pray the Jesus Prayer daily, "Lord Jesus, Son of God, have mercy on me, the sinner."

No one welcomes the pain we experience in grieving. In fact, we resent such pain. Yet, by God's grace, such pain can turn out to be the very occasion of spiritual growth. It can purge sin and develop character. It can deepen our trust in God. It can cure pride. It can give us a truer perspective on life. The pain of grief remains, but it is now transformed and even redeemed, as God uses it as a tool to deepen our faith and draw us closer to Him.

St. Isaac the Syrian once wrote, "In your heart be always ready for your departure. If you are wise, you will expect it at every hour... Go to sleep with these thoughts every night, and reflect upon them every day. 'When the messenger comes, go joyfully to meet him, saying, 'Come in peace. I knew that you would be here and I have not neglected anything that could help me on my journey'."

Pain is God's megaphone. He whispers to us in our pleasures. He speaks to us in our conscience. He shouts to us in our suffering.

~ *C.S. Lewis*

"She should have seen the doctor sooner." "He should never have done that." You may be totally right. Yet, after quality mourning, to keep clinging to the "shoulds" draped around that loss does block healing.

Offload Your Grief Onto God

The Apostle Peter writes in his letter, "Cast all your anxieties on him, for he cares about you" (1 Pet. 5:7).

Commenting on this verse J.B. Phillips writes,

In one sense it is quite plain that God wants us to be permanently immature. But there is a sense in which the conscientious (person)... can be overburdened... Such over-anxiety can be 'offloaded' onto God, for each one of us is his personal concern... The word used for 'casting' is an almost violent word, conveying the way in which a man at the end of his tether might throw aside an intolerable burden. And the Christian is recommended to throw this humanly insupportable weight upon the only One who can bear it and at the same time to realize that God cares for him intimately as a person. 'He careth for you' is hardly strong enough, and I don't know that I did much better rendering the words, "You are his personal concern"... It may seem strange to us, and it may seem an idea quite beyond our little minds to comprehend, but each one of us matters to God.

Here then is the basis, the foundation, on which relinquishment stands: faith in a God who loves and cares for each one of us personally.

May we bring our grief each day to the One who is utterly acquainted with sorrow; to the Man of sorrows Who truly cares for us. You matter to him!

Death is nothing at all... I have only slipped, away into the next room. Whatever we were to each other, that we are still. Call me by my old familiar name, speak to me in the easy way which you always used to. Laugh as we always laughed at the little jokes we enjoyed together. Play, smile, think of me, pray for me. Let my name be the household word that it always was. Let it be spoken without effort. Life means all that it ever meant. It is the same as it ever was; there is absolutely unbroken continuity. Why should I be out of your mind because I am out of your sight? I am but waiting for you, for an interval, somewhere very near just around the corner. All is well. Nothing is past; nothing is lost. One brief moment and all will be as it was before – only better, infinitely happier forever – we will all be one together with Christ.

~ *S. Russell*

When it gets darkest, the stars come out.

When the bee steals from a flower, it also fertilizes that flower.

~ *Charles A. Beard*

Turn Your Loved One Over to God

The prayer of relinquishment can be most helpful when we lose a loved one. We tend to be very possessive about our loved ones. We feel they belong solely to us. We forget that we are all God's children, that we belong to Him not just during this short life but for all eternity. Often, when a loved one dies, we refuse to let go. We refuse to accept the death. We refuse to let God take the loved one. We rebel. The result is that we never adjust and we make ourselves miserable. The relinquishment that is born of faith would say at such a moment, "Dear Lord, You were the One who gave me my beloved son or father or relative. I thank you for letting him live with us for the years that he did. Now that he has died, I shall not hold on to him; I shall let You take him to heaven. You have great plans for him in that other world. I turn him over to your great love and care." This kind of relinquishment has great healing power and provides a strong answer to the grief of bereavement.

When death comes, let go. Life is not ours. It is God's. Let Him take it back that He may give us more of it, infinitely more. For it is in dying that we are born to eternal life.

Turn to me and be gracious to me, for I am lonely and afflicted. Relieve the troubles of my heart, and bring me out of my distress. Consider my affliction and my trouble, and forgive all my sins.

~ Psalm 25:16-18

Can a mother forget the baby at her breast and have not compassion for the child she has borne? Though she may forget, I will not forget you! See, I have engraved you on the palms of my hands.

~ *Isaiah 49:15-16a*

Losses are multiple: the person is gone, the role is gone, the lifestyle is gone, known stresses are gone, securities are gone, dependencies left dangling unattached.

~ *D. Briggs*

Drink Christ, for He is the vine.
Drink Christ, for He is the rock from which water gushed.
Drink Christ, for He is the fountain of life.
Drink Christ, for He is the river whose current brings joy to the city of God.
Drink Christ, for He is peace.
Drink Christ, for streams of living water flow from His body.
Drink Christ, and drink the blood by which you were redeemed.
Drink Christ and drink His words.

~ *St. Ambrose of Milan*

Leave Your Grief with Him

The prayer of relinquishment can be of great help to us in overcoming our grief. A story is told of how one Christian managed to bear his anxieties. He was asked by a visitor: "I don't see how you could bear all the sorrow you've known in your lifetime."

"The Lord bore it for me," the Christian replied.

"Yes," said the visitor, "it is true that we must take our troubles to the Lord."

"We must do more than that," said the Christian. "We must leave them there with Him. Most people take their burdens to Him, but they bring them away with them, and are just as worried and unhappy as ever. But I take mine and I leave them with Him, and come away and forget them. And if the worry comes back, I take it to Him again; and I do this over and over, until at last I forget I have any worries, and am at peace."

A certain woman has a file called "God's Business." When there is something over which she has no control, she writes it out and files it. At the end of the year she opens the file and reads the entries. Sure enough. God took care of everything. Worry solves nothing.

Take your grief to the Lord each day. Express it in words and tears, but don't take it back with you. Drop the burden before His seat of mercy. Leave it there. If it comes back, do the same again.

Cancer is so limited...
It cannot cripple love,
It cannot shatter hope,
It cannot corrode faith,
It cannot eat away peace,
It cannot destroy confidence,
It cannot kill friendship,
It cannot shut out memories,
It cannot silence courage,
It cannot invade the soul,
It cannot reduce eternal life,
It cannot quench the Spirit,
It cannot lessen the power of the resurrection.

~ *D. Richardson*

My beloved, never-sick-a-day father dropped dead without warning. He was so young; a high soul; it was not fair! My world spun. I remember waking the next morning furious that the sun dared to be sparkling the day after his death. In my magical child thinking, because I was in total mourning, I felt that at least the day could have been cloudy. But life went on while I reeled inwardly for a good two years.

~ *D. Briggs*

Grief unexpressed is like a powder keg waiting to be ignited.

~ *J. Tatelbaum*

What Hurts Me?

There is a story of a rabbi sitting in his study. Suddenly his reading is interrupted by a knock on the door.

"Come in."

It was one of his students who was so grateful for his teacher he simply had to come and tell him.

"I just wanted you to know, Rabbi, how much I love you."

The rabbi put down his book and looked over his glasses. "What hurts me?"

The student looked at him quizzically. "What?" he asked.

"What hurts me?" the rabbi asked again.

The boy stood there, speechless. Finally shrugging his shoulders, he said, "I don't know."

"How can you love me," the rabbi asked, "if you don't know what hurts me?"

What hurts you? Do the people who love you know it? If not, how can they truly help you? How can we love one another if we don't know what hurts us? Have we ever told people what hurts us? We must!

Three times I (Paul) besought the Lord about this (suffering) that it should leave me; but he said to me, "My grace is sufficient for you, for my power is made perfect in weakness..." For the sake of Christ, then, I am content with weakness, insults, hardships, persecutions, and calamities; for when I am weak, then I am strong.

~ 2 Corinthians 12:8-9,10

An ancient proverb says, "All sunshine and no rain makes a desert." The Lord is at work in your life. The rain that is falling will yield a crop of beautiful flowers in the garden of your soul.

Grief is a passion, something that happens to us, something to endure. We can be stricken with it, we can be victims of it, we can be stuck in it. Or, we can meet it, get through it, and become quiet victors through the honest and courageous process of grieving.

~ A.R. Bozarth

God Uses Our Brokenness

Like a tree that is fertilized by its broken branches, God uses our brokenness for our growth. Just as God takes broken soil and produces a crop, broken clouds and produces rain, broken grain and produces bread, so He takes broken people like the Apostle Peter, weeping bitterly, broken by sin, and makes him a saint, a vessel to be used for God's greater glory.

"The Lord is near to the broken hearted and saves the crushed in spirit," we read in Psalm 34:18. The Lord is never as near to us as when we are broken and crushed. He takes the broken things of our life and makes them into the better things of His divine purposes. As one saint said, "I offered Jesus a broken heart; He took it and gave me a new and beautiful life." Broken to be more beautiful, more saintly, more holy, more humble, more understanding, more sensitive, more open to God's grace.

The brokenness we experience in grief will help us taste the sweetness of God's comfort.

Eric is gone, here and now, he is gone. Now I cannot talk with him, now I cannot see him, now I cannot hug him, now I cannot hear of his plans for the future. That is my sorrow.

~ *Nicholas Wolterstorff*

Plastic Garbage Bags

A widow said once,

It was almost ten months after my husband died before I could bring myself to give his clothes to Goodwill. And this, of course, triggered bitter tears, tears when I emptied his closet and drawers, tears when I folded everything and stuffed it into the big black plastic garbage bags, tears when the Goodwill man came to take the bags away. It was shattering, heart-wrenching, to see his life packed up in a bunch of plastic garbage bags.

Is this what life is all about in the end? Plastic garbage bags? Not if we have given to God that which we cannot keep in order to gain that which we cannot lose, not if we live in Christ and for Christ. Then the end of life will not consist of plastic garbage bags. It will be Jesus inviting us home with the words, "Come, O blessed of my Father, inherit the kingdom prepared for you from the foundation of the world" (Matt. 25:34).

Broken to be More Beautiful

Many years ago the architect planned that the walls of the Royal Palace be covered with sheets of beautiful mirrors from Paris. But when the shipment of glass arrived from Paris every mirror had been smashed in travel. The entire shipment was destroyed! The entrance could not be completed. Just as the workmen started gathering the broken pieces together to discard them the architect said, "Wait a minute. I've got an idea!" He then took them up in his hands and walked over to the entry. The skilled architect then put some glue on the wall and arranged the tiny pieces. He did this several times until he had an enormous distortion in reflections, sparkling with a rainbow of brilliant colors! At no point were they broken alike and at no point was the angle exact. Today, the Royal Palace is a dazzling brilliant display of prisms, reflecting light! As I read this story I could only think of one line: "Broken to be more beautiful!"

God takes the broken things in our lives, as the architect took the broken pieces of those mirrors and makes them over into the better things of his divine purpose. God can do wonders with a broken heart and a broken life if we will give Him the pieces. But this is exactly what most of us refuse to do: take the pieces to Him! I love the proverb which says, "God can draw straight even with crooked lines."

He can use your grief to help build a better you, if you will bring the pieces to Him.

Not every broken thing is irreparably hurt by its wound.
Sometimes broken things yield a hidden splendor.
The crushed flower yields perfume.
Only you know, Lord, what great good
May soon break
From my brokenheartedness,
If only I bring the pieces to you.

Blessed be the God and Father of our Lord Jesus Christ, the
Father of mercies and God of all comfort, who comforts us in
all our afflictions, so that we may be able to comfort those who
are in any affliction, with the comfort with which we ourselves
are comforted by God.

~ 2 Corinthians 1:3-4

A dear friend of mine was once driven by grief to do the work
of three people to burn off her pain through physical exertion.
She told me how she scrubbed her kitchen floor in the middle
of the night with tears streaming into the wash bucket, working
her muscles into exhaustion, before she could finally rest in a
deep sleep.

Cultivate the Awareness of God's Presence

The best antidote to grief available to all of us is the knowledge that God is with us.

Archbishop Anthony Bloom tells of one of the first people to seek his advice after ordination. She was an elderly woman who claimed, "I have been praying almost unceasingly for fourteen years and I have never had any sense of God's presence." Bloom discovered the woman's prayer time consisted mostly of her talking to God so he advised her to set aside fifteen minutes a day to "sit and just knit before the face of God." Later, the woman reported that when she tried to converse with God she felt nothing but when she sat quietly, placing herself deliberately in the presence of God, she felt wrapped in God's presence.

Recently I read one author's interesting suggestion on prayer which I think is particularly helpful. If you are going through troubled times in your own life, he suggests finding a nice easy chair, sitting down in a very relaxed fashion and then thinking about relaxing every muscle in your body, until you are completely relaxed. Then, think about the promises of God – that He will keep you in perfect peace, whose mind is stayed upon Him; that He will work all things together for your good; that He will bless you. Finally, claim all those promises until they soothe and assuage your soul. Then having put your body at ease and rest and claiming the peace of God for your soul, begin to ask Him for whatever it is that is on your heart.

Grief can be disarmed and conquered when you stop to remember that you are not alone. Wrap yourself up in God's presence each day.

Romano Guardini wrote about placing ourselves in God's presence each day:

God turns His face to man and thereby gives Himself to man... To be seen by Him... (is) to be enfolded in the deepest care... We are seen by Him whether we want to be or not. The difference is whether we try to elude His sight, or strive to enter into it.

None of the shortcomings and evil in our lives are fatal as long as they confront His gaze. The very act of placing ourselves in His sight is the beginning of renewal...

One of the aspects of prayer that is greatly emphasized by the Holy Fathers is the practice of the presence of God. St. Theophan the Recluse writes:

The essential part is to dwell in God, and this walking before God means that you live with the conviction ever before your consciousness that God is in you, as He is in everything; you live in the firm assurance that He sees all that is within you, knowing you better than you know yourself. This awareness of the eyes of God looking in your inner being... searching your soul and your heart, seeing all that is there... is the most powerful lever in the mechanism of the inner spiritual life.

My First Christmas Without David

A father writes about his first Christmas without his 25-year-old son who was suddenly struck dead by lightning.

A time when I felt most vulnerable were the days prior to our first Christmas after Dave's death. For weeks I had been told how festive seasons intensify one's grief. Christmas for some is a time they wish they could avoid.

For me it became an opposite experience, but it did not start that way. The day before Christmas, when Irene and I stood at Dave's grave, I was overwhelmed by the realization that a graveyard would always be part of our Christmas – this sacred, happy family time. We sang several songs with Irene carrying the tune, because my eyes were blurred with tears and my whole being bowed over in sobbing. Then we prayed, thanking God for Dave. Again I was overwhelmed by the sense of loss, with our son gone and in a grave.

When we began our festive Christmas Eve dinner, sur- rounded by sons, daughters-in-law, and grandchildren, I felt as though I had been cleansed by the tears. Others felt the same cleansing and were free to talk about Dave as though he were present. For me Christmas was a time when I gave Dave back to God. I reflected this in the closing prayer I gave at our dinner:

"Father in heaven, this night is especially sacred, tender, and fraught with meaning for us. David's chair stands empty; his plate carries no food. He is with You, with the angels, with the many loved ones who are part of the cloud of witnesses looking at us from the other side of life. You

know how we miss him – how easily our tears flow. The
depths of feeling we experience tonight cannot be expressed
in words.

"In the midst of our tears we cling fiercely to Your word.
And because we do, we believe David continues to live, to
serve, to sing, to talk, to remember, to see, and significantly,
to love us still. Though our eyes cannot see him, O God, we
believe he sees us, hears us, loves us more than ever. Give
us an increased sense of reality as to his presence with us.
Increase our confidence in Your promises.

"I confess, dear God, that I have held on to Dave as
though he belonged to us. He is Yours, because we gave him
to You in Holy Baptism."[2]

I need not tell you with what anxiety I await better news from
you. Since death (take my words literally) is the true goal of
our lives, I have made myself so well acquainted with this true
and best friend of man that the idea of it no longer has terrors
for me, but rather much that is tranquil and comforting. And I
thank God that He has granted me the good fortune to obtain
the opportunity of regarding death as the key to our happiness.
I never lie down in bed without considering that, young as I
am, perhaps on the morrow I may be no more. Yet not one of
those who know me could say that I am morose or melancholy,
and for this I thank my Creator daily, and wish heartily that the
same happiness may be given to my fellow men.

~ *Mozart*

2 *Five Cries of Grief.* Merton P. Strommen and A. Irene Strommen. Harper Collins Publishers. New York, N.Y. 1993.

Living in the Future

Some people live in the past; others in the future. "How strange it is, our little procession of life!" wrote Stephen Leacock. "The child says, 'When I grow up!' And grown-up, he says, 'When I get married'. Then the thought changes to 'When I'm able to retire'. And when retirement comes, he looks back over the landscape traversed; a cold wind seems to sweep over it; somehow he has missed it all, and it is gone. Life, we learn too late, is in the living, in the tissue of every day and hour."

Father Elchaninov writes, "Either we look back sadly on the past or live in the expectation of a future in which, it seems to us, real life will begin. But the present – that is, what actually is our life – is spent in these fruitless dreams and regrets."[3]

One can take a flashlight and flash the light so far in front that one will not be able to see what is on the path immediately in front. Sometimes we can focus so much on the paths of tomorrow that we falter and fall on the path of today. Someone said so well, "First do the good you know; then the good that you do not know will be shown to you."

The best way to cope with grief is not to look to the past or be anxious about the future, but to trust God who gives us life one day at a time and promises to give us "our daily bread," our much-needed comfort, strength and sustenance for each day.

---

3 *Diary of a Russian Priest*. Alexander Elchaninov. SVS Press. Crestwood, N.Y. 1982.

Sunglasses for Grief

Try not to embrace your grief alone. If there is ever a time when we need true friends, it is when we lose a loved one. We need friends who will allow us to express our grief freely through mourning. We need friends who will encourage us to speak about our departed loved one. We need friends who will say, "It must be tragically painful to lose a spouse of so many years. Tell me about it." One cannot heal without mourning or expressing one's grief outwardly. Following is a useful analogy:

When you go out on a sunny day, the bright sunlight on your unprotected eyes creates stress. It makes seeing difficult. Sunglasses help filter out the harmful sunrays. Maybe you can think of the stress of your grief in just that way. If you respond to the stress of the death of someone loved alone, or without sunglasses, you may be overwhelmed. But if you accept the help of other people, just like putting on the sunglasses, your work of mourning will be accomplished more easily, and with less damage to yourself.

Loss is like going through the birth canal. You are squeezed, pushed, disoriented, thrust from known to the unknown. It is pitch dark. But you are in process. You will be asked to function quite anew. The impossible dream lies ahead. The Light does come.

~ D. Briggs

God Gives Grace for Each Day

People miss the joy of the present because they live in the future. We can make plans for tomorrow. We can have hope for tomorrow. But it is wrong for us to borrow tomorrow's trouble, which may never come, and to add it to our burden for today. "The load of tomorrow added to today makes even the strongest falter," said Carlyle. There will be trouble enough in the tomorrows, but there will also be God's grace and strength to help us meet those troubles. "Therefore do not be anxious about tomorrow," said Jesus, "for tomorrow will be anxious for itself. Let the day's own trouble be sufficient for the day" (Matt. 6:34).

When a high school student was given his algebra book at the beginning of the school year, he glanced at the last chapter and saw some of the complex problems which he couldn't even begin to solve. He was ready to give up on the course. But as the school year progressed, he learned that if he took the book chapter by chapter and day by day did his work diligently, then, when he came to the difficult problems at the end of the book, he will have developed the skill to be able to solve them.

The best thing about the future is that it is offered to us by God a day at a time. God will lead us through the grief process one step at a time.

It is dangerous to try to take shortcuts through it. God has important lessons for us to learn as He leads us through the process of grief one step at a time, one day at a time, and one prayer at a time.

Any man can do his work, however hard, just for today. Any man can rise above resentment just for a day. Any alcoholic can stop drinking just for today. Any man can live patiently just for a day. Any man can fight the battle of grief for just one day. It is when we try to carry the burdens of yesterday and our fears for tomorrow that we break down.

If all the weight that was to pass over a bridge in a year was placed on it all at the same time, it would collapse – but it survives because the weight is placed on the bridge one day at a time. John Wanamaker said once, "One may walk over the highest mountain – one step at a time."

If my question is, "How can this happen to me?" distress and anguish follow. If my question is, "What lesson can I learn from this?" growth and renewal follow. What is your question? Yesterday's disaster is today's teacher if we linger past the pain to learn the lesson.

~ *D. Briggs*

Do Something in Memory of Your Loved One

An old man got on a bus on February 14 carrying a dozen red roses. He sat beside a young man. The young man looked at the roses and said, "Somebody's going to get a beautiful Valentine's Day gift."

"Yes," said the old man.

A few minutes went by and the old man noticed that his young companion was staring at the roses. "Do you have a girl-friend?" the old man asked.

"I do," said the young man. "I'm going to see her now. I'm taking her this." He held up a Valentine's Day card.

They rode along in silence for another ten minutes, and the old man rose to get off the bus. As he stepped out into the aisle, he suddenly placed the roses on the young man's lap and said, "I think my wife would want you to have these. I'll tell her that I gave them to you."

He left the bus quickly, and as the bus pulled away, the young man turned to see the old man enter the gates of a cemetery.

One of the most healing things for grief is to do something in memory of your loved one. Examples include volunteering for hospital work, assisting at a food shelter, participating in Meals on Wheels, establishing a church grief support group, contributing to medical research, or funding a scholarship. Such projects contribute greatly to the healing of grief. They allow the light that your loved one brought into this world to continue to shine.

Helpful Suggestions

- Everyone needs some help – don't be afraid to accept it.
- While you may feel pressured to put on a brave front, it is important to make your needs known by expressing your feelings to those you trust.
- Often numbness sees us through the first few days or weeks. Don't be too surprised if a let-down comes later.
- Many people are more emotionally upset during bereavement than at any other time in their lives and are frightened by this. Be aware that severe upset is not unusual and if you are alarmed, seek a professional opinion.
- Whether you feel you need to be alone or accompanied – make it known. Needing company is common and does not mean you will always be dependent on it.
- There is no set time limit for grieving. It varies from person to person, depending on individual circumstances.

We never lose a true love. Their impact on our lives is irrevocably with us always. Remember that as you mourn your dear one. They are always as close as your memory. They have left a precious piece of themselves with you forever.

~ *D. Briggs*

Confessions of an Oncology Nurse

An oncology nurse writes:

I am an oncology (cancer) nurse, which often has meant caring for and caring about people who are dying. People often ask me how I can stand to work with dying people, saying, "It must be so depressing." I honestly tell them that I almost always feel it is a privilege and that I am lucky to be able to work with the dying. To me, many other types of work would be much more depressing – working at the IRS comes to mind (my apologies to those working there). I'm lucky to work with the dying, because they are the ones who are really living. They very rarely get bent out of shape over the stock market, or car repairs, or laundry that needs to be done, or any of the other countless frustrations over which those of us who are "well" spend our time fussing and fuming. Talk about perspective! These people are concerned with the very basic elements of human existence, and there's no time or energy for trivialities.

So... I definitely can stand to work with the dying. What I couldn't stand is caring for and caring about these people and then watching them die if I didn't have the personal belief that this earthly existence is just part of our soul's journey with God. If I didn't believe that the Lord would open our graves and raise us up in whatever way that we as mortals cannot understand, I couldn't possibly live and work as I do. So many that I have known and loved are now gone from this realm, but I have no doubt that they are with us still, in big and small ways, and that my soul will be with them again, in another realm.

You Are Married to Your Friends

Katherine Graham once said, "When you live alone, you are married to your friends." It is a clinically proven fact that people with plentiful social support are less likely to suffer from anxiety and depression. It is important for those who are grieving to stay closely connected with family and friends.

Elva and Irma would testify to this. Five years after Irma's daughter died, her husband was killed in a tractor accident. Elva immediately went to Irma's side and helped her in any way she could. "She practically lived here for a while," Irma said.

When Elva's husband died, Irma stayed close to her side. Elva's doctor recommended she get counseling for the bereaved. But Elva told him she really didn't need any of that because she had Irma. "I know she will always be there for me." They are both 84 years old and do many things together, including traveling. "When you live alone, you are married to your friends." How true!

Turn to me and be gracious to me, for I am lonely and afflicted. Relieve the troubles of my heart, and bring me out of my distress.

~ Psalm 25:16-17

A Welcoming Committee in Heaven

In my fifty years in the priesthood I have had occasion often to be at the side of people who were dying. What I have discovered is that very often the person who is dying will begin calling out the names of loved ones in his family who have preceded him in death, talking to them as if they were present. Some believe that somehow our loved ones in heaven are informed in advance when one of their own on earth is about to join them. They spread the word around like wild fire saying, "Guess what? So-and-So is about to join us." And they joyfully set up a welcoming committee so that when we leave this life, we are immediately met and welcomed not only by our precious Lord Jesus but also by our loved ones in heaven amid shouts of joy and jubilation.

There is a true story of a grandmother who was dying. She was in a coma. Unbeknownst to her, her oldest grandchild, 17 years old, was suddenly killed in an accident. Her son, Bob, the father of the deceased grandson, had just returned from the funeral. He sat by her bed holding her hand. The grandmother, in a coma, knew nothing of her grandson's death or the funeral.

Suddenly her eyes opened. There was a far-off look in them, as if she was seeing beyond the room. A look of wonder passed over her face. "I see Jesus," she exclaimed, adding, "why there's Father... and there's Mother..."

And then,

"And there's Robby! I didn't know Robby died..."

Robby, of course, was her 17-year-old grandson. Her hand patted her son's knee gently. "Poor Bob..." she said softly, and was gone. Bob, of course, was her son, sitting by the bed, whose son Robby had just died. This is a true story and it shows how the welcoming committee was there to receive her: the Lord Jesus, her father, her mother and Robby!

Have you not known? Have you not heard?
The Lord is the everlasting God, the Creator of the ends of the
    earth.
He does not faint or grow weary, his understanding is
    unsearchable.
He gives power to the faint, and to him who has no might he
    increases strength,
Even youths shall faint and be weary, and young men shall fall
    exhausted;
but they who wait for the Lord shall renew their strength, they
    shall mount up with wings like eagles,
they shall run and not be weary, they shall walk and not faint.

~ Isaiah 40:28-31

A few years ago I had the privilege of celebrating the divine liturgy in the empty tomb of Jesus in the Church of the Resurrection in Jerusalem. It was an experience I shall never forget. It was an experience of "beholding" the resurrection with the eyes of faith as I saw Jesus risen in me as I had never seen Him before. I thought of the beautiful words of St. Gregory Nazianzus, "Yesterday I was crucified with Him; today I am glorified with Him. Yesterday I died with Him; today I am made alive in Him. Yesterday I was buried with Him; today I rise with Him."

~ A.C.

"We" Experiences in Life

The truly committed Christian is one who has crossed out the "I." And when you cross out the "I," you have a cross which is also a plus sign. This results in a partnership: God plus I equals: We.

For example, a certain person beset by many problems was unable to sleep one night. In his sleeplessness he found himself saying in despair,

"O God, what shall I do?" As he kept saying these words, he found they suddenly became, "O God, what shall *we* do?" He realized suddenly that God had spoken to him through his own words. From that moment on he became aware of the fact that he was never alone, that God was involved in the problems of his life. From that time on the question was never, "What shall I do?" but rather, "What shall we do, Lord?"

Isn't that what we need more of in life? A lot less "I" and a lot more "We." We have two options before us. We can face life alone and say, "I have so many temptations. I have so many problems. So many difficult decisions to make. I have another hard day ahead of me. I have to live with so many difficult people." Or, we can face each day in partnership with the Lord Jesus and say, "We have a full day before us, Lord. We will face it together. We will face its trials, its problems, its joys, its sorrows together."

When we consciously invite Christ into our life in prayer each day and let Him take control, we lead a "we" life.

The Icon of the Falling Asleep of the Theotokos

The icon of the Falling Asleep of the Theotokos expresses a powerful truth that helps us cope with grief. The icon portrays the body of Mary in a coffin. Above her, inside a radiant ray of light, stands the Lord Jesus, holding his mother's soul, pictured as a babe in swaddling clothes, to denote her birth through death, into a new and eternal life with God. We gain an important Christian understanding of death through this beautiful icon. When we die, the body falls asleep in the Lord and is placed in a cemetery. The word cemetery comes from the Greek word *koimitirion*, which means a place where one sleeps. The body will indeed sleep there until the Second Coming of Jesus. The soul, however, is taken to heaven by Jesus, exactly as Jesus is seen in this icon, embracing and carrying His mother's soul with Him to heaven.

So where is our loved one who has died? The answer is: in the embrace of Jesus just as His mother's soul is in His embrace in this lovely icon. At the Second Coming, Jesus will raise (awaken) the buried (sleeping) body and re-unite it with the soul. Thus, shall we ever be with the Lord.

If you have lost a loved one recently, how comforting it is to realize that your loved one is now in the embrace of Jesus. How effectively this icon helps express our Orthodox Christian belief about death which is now a defeated enemy, thanks to the Resurrection of Jesus. "Christ has risen from the dead, by His death He has destroyed death, and to those in the tombs (to your beloved loved one) He has bestowed life."

Easing the Pain of Loss

Following are some ways by which we can ease the pain of loss.

- Accept the help of others. Develop a support system.
- Don't expect miracles overnight. You must go through the hard work of expressing your grief which takes from one to two years.
- Resume your daily routine. Having a routine helps heal grief.
- Through prayer and the reading of God's word, fill your mind each day with God's healing promises.
- Take advantage of a grief support group in your area.
- Don't compare yourself with others. Grief is unique with each person. Some persons heal sooner, others later.
- Don't be afraid to express your feelings. They are not abnormal. Death generates intense feelings that are a natural part of bereavement.
- Forget "normal" for a while. Death turns life upside down for a brief period.
- Pamper yourself during this period. Be tolerant of your physical and emotional limits.
- Avoid people who frustrate you in your recovery from grief.
- Educate yourself about grief. Visit a bookstore or library. Select a book on the grieving process that will help you.
- Don't make any major changes in your life for one to two years unless absolutely necessary.
- Know where and when to get help. Stay in touch with your priest and doctor.
- Talk about your grief openly.

- Treasure your memories. Share them. Take out old photo albums and share the memories with your family and friends.
- Grief is a process not an event. Be patient with yourself. It will take time.
- Crying is God's way of releasing internal tension in your body. It is one of the excretory processes, such as sweating and exhaling, that involve the removal of waste products from the body. It is not a sign of weakness. It is an indication that you are doing the "work of mourning."

Suffering cannot be "justified"; but it can be used, accepted – and through this acceptance, transfigured.

~ *Bishop Kallistos Ware*

Christianity does not explain suffering; it shows us what to do with it.

~ *Baron Von Hugel*

Temporal losses are not spiritual losses, and trouble, sadness, pain, and sickness are the language of divine providence, its secret code, which when deciphered in the Spirit spell resurrection, joy, and eternal glory.

~ *Matthew the Poor*

If No Tears, The Body Will Weep

Medical science tells us that if the eyes do not weep to provide relief, the body will begin to weep. Ulcers, migraines, colitis and a hundred other nervous disorders may be no more than the body attempting to release in other ways what God intends us to express through tears. As Dickens had Mr. Bumble say in *Oliver Twist*, "It opens the lungs, washes the countenance, exercises the eyes, and softens down the temper, so cry away." Crying depressurizes us emotionally. It relieves stresses that can affect our bodies.

The Bible is surely no stranger to crying. There is even a book in the Bible that sounds like one great sob – the Book of Lamentations.

I remember walking alone one day shortly after my wife's death and crying buckets. As this was happening, I asked myself, "Where is God in all of this?" And I suddenly realized that God was right there in those tears. Those God-given tears were God's healing agent for my grief. They were providing release for my deep grief.

When analyzed chemically tears of grief are found to contain a substance not found in other kinds of tears. Whatever the substance, it contributes greatly to the healing of grief. "Blessed are those who express their grief through mourning, for they shall be comforted," said Jesus.

When pleasant times cease, and we are besieged by bad news – a death, an accident, a moral lapse, a defeat, a frightening doctor's report, loss of a job – we must not panic and say, "Where is God now?" He is where he was in pleasant days, at the other end of the telephone line.

In such times, if we listen closely, our phone is ringing. God is calling. He is saying to us, "I am as near as breathing. Keep talking to me. My grace is still sufficient."

~ *A. Halvorson*

God did not say, "You will not be tempted. You will not labor hard. You will not be troubled." But God did say, "You will not be overcome."

~ *Julian of Norwich*

But we have this treasure in earthen vessels, to show that the transcendent power belongs to God and not to us. We are afflicted in every way, but not crushed; perplexed, but not driven to despair; persecuted, but not forsaken; struck down, but not destroyed; always carrying in the body the death of Jesus, so that the life of Jesus may also be manifested in our bodies.

~ *2 Corinthians 4:7-10*

Tears: A Gift of God

Tears are a gift of God. St. John Climacus said, "God in His love for mankind gave us tears." In fact, the gift of tears is one of the 30 rungs on the famous ladder to heaven of St. John Climacus.

I like the sign that appeared at a supermarket checkout counter in San Antonio, Texas. It said, "English and Spanish spoken here. Tears understood." Who doesn't understand tears?

One of the peculiar customs of North American culture is the restrictions it places on crying.

This stoic determination to maintain a stiff upper lip makes life more difficult than it need be. We believe it important to oil a motor regularly to keep it running smoothly. Well, tears are the lubricant of the spirit. They ease the meshing of our emotional gears. They clear away the grime and pain. They release the bitterness and perplexity stored up inside us. Of course there is weeping which is neurotic and needs the attention of a psychiatrist. But most of us have the opposite problem. We need to be assured, and to assure others, that it's okay to cry.

Grief is not a problem to be solved; it is an expression of the fact that I loved someone and still love that someone. If this is so, then no one has the right to tell me when to stop grieving. I must embrace that love and express it through tears of mourning. That is how God brings healing.

How much longer must I endure grief in my soul, and sorrow in my heart by day and by night?

~ *Psalm 13:2*

Take pity on me, Yahweh, I am in trouble now. Grief wastes away my eye, my throat, my inward parts. For my life is worn out with sorrow, my years with sighs.

~ *Psalm 31:9-10*

Death is not extinguishing the light, but putting out the lamp because the dawn has come.

~ *Rabindranath Tagore*

My tears are the words with which I tell God of my pain.

~ *Adolfo Quezada*

Live a Connected Life

Nothing gets anywhere until it is connected. A horse never pulls until it is connected, harnessed. Steam never drives anything until it is channeled, connected. No human life ever produces until it is connected to the power of God.

The electric outlet on the wall is a source of tremendous power. It can produce heat and light, cut down trees, brew coffee, toast bread, mow lawns, open cans, turn on radios, refrigerate and freeze food, cook meals, etc., but first we must plug in; we must connect with the source of power.

There is no greater source of power than God. We connect with that power through faith, prayer, and the sacraments. Faith is like the link on the freight car that connects with the locomotive. Prayer is not only conversation with God; it is hearing the knock of Jesus on the door of our soul and opening to let Him in. It is meditating on the all-powerful name of Jesus through the Jesus Prayer until the heart swallows the Lord and the Lord the heart. It is a constant *epiclesis*, or prayer that God the Holy Spirit may come to dwell in us with His wisdom and power. We connect by feeding on the Bread of Life – God's word – each day as we read His personal letter to us, the Holy Bible. We connect when we receive Him penitently and prayerfully in the Eucharist: "He who eats My flesh and drinks My blood abides in Me and I in him" (John 6:54).

It is by maintaining our life-giving connection to God that we shall find the strength to overcome grief.

Come, Let Us Bestow the Final Kiss

Metropolitan Anthony of Sourozh wrote,

In the Orthodox Church we bring the dead person to the church as soon as we can. We pray in the presence of an open coffin. Adults and children approach it. Death is not something to be hidden: it is something simple and a part of life. And the children can look into the face of the departed person and see the peace which has come upon it. We give a kiss to the departed person This is the moment when we must not forget to warn the child that when he or she kisses the forehead of a person that was always warm, it will be cold and we can say, "This is the mark of death." Life goes with warmth. Death is cold. And then the child is not horrified, because it has experience of things cold and things warm, and each of them has its own nature, each of them has its own meaning.

These first impressions determine how we confront death later on.

Come let us bestow the final kiss to the one death has taken, who has now departed from us, and proceeds to his resting place, no longer troubled over the things of this world... As we part let us pray that the Lord grant him eternal rest.

~ From the Orthodox Funeral Service

Enveloped by God's Presence

God's presence is ever about us.

- "Lo, I am with you always," said Jesus (Matt. 28:20).
- Elsewhere He says, "The Kingdom of God is within you" (1 Cor. 3:16).
- Paul says that God is closer than the air we breathe for "in Him we live and move and have our being" (Acts 17:28).
- The Psalmist sings: "Whither shall I go from thy Spirit? Or whither shall I flee from thy presence? If I ascend to heaven, thou art there! If I take the wings of the morning and dwell in the uttermost parts of the sea, even there thy hand shall lead me, and thy right hand shall hold me" (Ps. 139:7-10).
- Yahweh, you examine me and know me, you know if I am standing or sitting, you read my thoughts from far away, whether I walk, lie down, you are watching, you know every detail of my conduct (Ps. 139:1-3).
- "When you pray, believe that God is near and hears. Say the prayer for God's ear alone... The essential thing is to stand consciously in the presence of the Lord, with fear, faith and love" (St. Theophan the Recluse).

We are truly enveloped by God's presence constantly. Stand in that presence each day. Claim it. You are not alone in your grief.

The Lord is my pace-setter, I shall not rush.
He makes me stop and rest for quiet intervals;
He provides me with images of stillness, which restore my serenity.
He leads me in the ways of efficiency through calmness of mind.
And His guidance is peace.
Even though I have a great many things to accomplish each day
I will not fret, for His Presence is here.
His timelessness, His all-importance will keep me in balance.
He prepares refreshment and renewal in the midst of my activity
By anointing my mind with His oils of tranquility.
My cup of joyous energy overflows.
Surely harmony and effectiveness shall be the fruit of my hours
For I shall walk in the pace of my Lord and dwell in His house forever.

~ Japanese version of the 23rd Psalm

H.A.L.T. – Never make any decisions when you are

*H*ungry,

*A*ngry,

*L*onely or

*T*ired.

Spread it Out Before the Lord

Prayer is giving all our thoughts to God, opening to Him the secret places that we guard so diligently. It is like Tevye in *Fiddler on the Roof* who, while talking to himself, is talking to God at the same time. He carries on a conversation with God sharing with him the aches and pains as well as the joys of his everyday life, even joking with Him. Another excellent example of prayer as a God-centered dialogue are the Psalms. David carries on a constant conversation with God in the Psalms. He lays bare his soul before Him.

In the Old Testament, Hezekiah received a disturbing letter from his enemy. It was the kind of letter to cause a person to lose his sleep for nights. But, Hezekiah having read the letter, "went up into the house of the Lord, and spread it out before the Lord." Whatever the invading anxiety or worry is, we can always "spread it out" before the Lord in prayer.

Take your grief to Jesus each day in prayer. Spread it all out before Him. He cares for you.

Cast your burden on the Lord, and he will sustain you.

~ Psalm 55:22

O Lord, we pray for our departed _____. We believe.
Lord, that whoever believes in You shall never die. Our loved
ones are now with You in a special place You have prepared for
them. We thank you for the years they were with us. Now, they
cannot come to us, but we will go to them. The separation is
only temporary. We look forward to the day when we shall be
reunited in your kingdom. We loved them, but You love them
infinitely more. We relinquish them to Your greater love and
care. May they rest safe in your gentle bosom, secure in Your
gentle arms. Grant us, the survivors, the strength each day to
endure and overcome the pain of grief. It is a pain we cannot
escape but with Your help we shall pass through it and come
away with greater empathy, understanding and sympathy. Amen.

Pour out your heart like water before the presence of the Lord.
~ Lamentations 2:19

I cry aloud to the Lord, and He answers me from His holy hill.
~ Psalm 3:4

Prayer is remembering to call home because you are a child of God.

The Serenity of Death

A child may be introduced to death in a monstrous way that
will make him morbid. What follows is a real example, not a parable. A beloved grandmother died after a long and painful illness. I
was summoned to the house, and when I arrived, I discovered that
the children had been removed. The parents explained, "We could
not allow the children to stay in a house where there was a dead
person." I replied, "Why not?"" "Because they know what death
is." "And what is death?" I asked.

"They saw a rabbit torn to pieces by a cat in the garden the
other day, so they know what death is." So I suggested that if
that was the image of death which these children had they were
bound all their lives to live with a sense of horror whenever
they heard the word death, whenever they attended a memorial
service, whenever they saw a coffin – untold horror hidden in a
wooden box.

After a long argument, during which the parents said to me
that the children were bound to become nervous wrecks if they
were allowed to see their grandmother and that their mental
condition would be my responsibility, I brought the children
back. Their first question was, "What really happened to
Granny?" I replied, "You have heard her say time and again
that she longed to join her husband in God's kingdom, where
he had already gone. Now it has happened to her."

"So she is happy?" said one of the children. I said, "Yes."
Then we went into the room where the grandmother lay. The
stillness was wonderful. The old lady, whose face had been rav-
aged by the last years of suffering, lay absolutely still and

serene. One of the children said, "So that is death." And the other one said, "How beautiful." Here are two forms of the same experience. Are we going to allow children to see death in terms of the little rabbit torn to pieces by cats in the garden, or are we going to let them see the serenity and beauty of death?[4]

~ Metropolitan Anthony of Sourozh

God makes silences in every life; the silence of sleep, the silence of sickness, the silence of sorrow, and then the last great silence of death. One of the hardest things in the world is to get little children to keep still. They are in a state of perpetual activity, restless, eager, questioning, alert. And just as a mother says to her child, be still and hushes it to sleep that it may rest, so God does sooner or later with all of us. What a quiet, still place the sick-room is! What a time for self-examination! What silence there is in a house where a loved one has died! How the voices are hushed, and every footstep soft. Had we the choosing of our own affairs we would never have chosen such an hour as that; and yet how often it is rich in blessing. All the activities of our years may not have taught us quite so much as we learned in the silences of sickness, sorrow and death. So God comes, in his irresistible way, which never ceases to be a way of love, and says, "Be still, and know that I am God."

4 *Death and Bereavement*. St. Stephen's Press. Oxford, England. 2002.

Mary Magdalene's Tears

The first recorded words of Jesus after His resurrection have to do with tears. They were the words He spoke to Mary Magdalene, "Woman, why are you weeping?" Mary was heartbroken, crushed, overcome with sorrow. Not only was Jesus dead, but now His body was missing. So she wept.

When Jesus asked, "Why are you weeping?" she answered, "Because they have taken away my Lord and I know not where they have laid Him. If you tell me, I shall take care of Him." She thought the person she was speaking to was a gardener.

Then Jesus spoke just one word to her. He spoke her name, "Mary."

This beautiful story tells me that when I weep tears of sorrow, I need to listen to hear the voice of Jesus speaking my name. If I am still and listen, I will hear it, not in an audible voice but in the quietness of the soul. The Risen Christ will come to comfort and console me. For the Christian, the time of sorrow is a bittersweet time in life. It is bitter because of the pain of loss and the suffering of separation. But it is also sweet in the experience of the nearness of God and the reality of His power. As someone said so well, "The soul can have no rainbow if the eyes have no tears."

God's strength behind you,
His concern for you,
His love within you, and
His arms beneath you are more than sufficient for the
job ahead of you.

~ *W.A. Ward*

"God is!
I am!
With Him
I can."

~N. *Wolf*

For to me to live is Christ, and to die is gain... I am hard
pressed between the two. My desire is to depart and be with
Christ, for that is far better.

~ *Philippians 1:21,23*

Something else which a person bereaved must learn never to do
is to speak of the love relationship that existed before in the
past tense. One should never say, "We loved one another." We
should always say, "We love each other." Love cannot be cor-
rupted by death. We cannot allow our love to become a thing of
the past without recognizing that this means that we do not
believe in the continuing life of the person who has died.

~ *Metropolitan Anthony of Sourozh*

Men Fare Worse than Women

Edward Dolnick, an American author, wrote:
After a spouse dies, men seem to fare worse than women. They are more depressed, more likely to fall ill and more likely to die. As a result nearly 80 percent of the population over 65 years old and living alone are women. Men fare poorly, it seems, because in many cases their wives were their sole confidantes. Without a spouse, new widowers flounder and sink. Women who lose a husband, in contrast, often have a circle of close friends to confide in and count on.

Our advice? Seek out friends and family. Reach out to them when you need them. Don't wait for them to guess your needs. Become part of a grief support group. Seek out someone who is willing to listen.

Though it may strike you as unnecessary, I want to remind you of the most essential bodily function in connection with grieving – breathing. It is the source of all life. Yet, when we are weighed heavily with the burden of strong and painful feelings, breathing is what we first forget to do.

"Keep breathing!"

You might breathe with a prayer or an affirmation in mind. For example, as you breathe in, say to yourself, "I am." And as you breathe out, say to yourself, "In God's hands."

"In am..."   "In God's hands."

~ A.R. Bozarth

Get involved. To have a friend, be one. Reach out rather than waiting to be reached out to.

Word Therapy

There is therapy to be found in words. Certain words agitate the mind, but other words contribute to peace of mind.

Words such as quietness, tranquility and imperturbability can produce a healing effect if repeated often enough and visualized as being absorbed into consciousness. Psychotherapists now use word therapy to help people who are anxious.

A superb source of word therapy can be found in God's precious promises if they are claimed with faith and repeated often. Here are some samples:

Thou wilt keep him in perfect peace whose mind is stayed on thee.

~ Isaiah 26:3

In quietness and confidence shall be your strength.

~ Isaiah 30:15

Come unto me, all ye that labor and are heavy laden, and I will give you rest.

~ Matthew 11:28

Peace I leave with you, my peace I give unto you: not as the world giveth, give I unto you. Let not your heart be troubled, neither let it be afraid.

~ John 14:27-28

Face the Storm

One mother whose son had died said to her pastor one day:
Some time after Mark died, during a particularly rough time, an image you used in another sermon brought me hope anew. Do you remember when you talked about sheep that are caught in a storm? When a storm comes up in the cold of winter, and the wind comes from behind the sheep and blows the icy rain under their wool, they will freeze to death. As the storm comes, the sheep must turn to face into storm. I do not suppose they choose to do that. You said that sheep are not very bright and must be carefully guided by the sheepdogs and shepherd. It is the shepherd and dogs that turn the sheep to face into the storm so that they will survive.

I saw then that that was what God was doing for me – turning me to face the storm, and staying with me so that I could live. What a marvelous image. What hope it brought in the hardest of days.

In all paths on which people must journey in this world they will find no peace unless they draw near to the hope which is in God.

~ St. Isaac the Syrian

Every place of pain is a place of revelation. "This illness is not unto death; it is for the glory of God, so that the Son of God may be glorified by means of it."

~ John 11:4

A Flicker of Light

Metropolitan Anthony of Sourozh wrote,
At the funeral service we stand with lighted candles (a Slavic practice). In this way we are proclaiming the Resurrection: we stand with lighted candles in the same way in which we stand in church during Easter night. But we also stand witnessing before God that this person brought at least a flicker of light into the twilight of the world, that this person has not lived in vain, and that we will keep, protect, increase, share out this light, so that it may illumine more and more people, so that it may grow thirtyfold, sixtyfold, a hundredfold. And if we set out to live in such a way, as to be the continuation of the earthly life of the departed person, if we set out to be the continuation of everything that was noble and good and true and holy in this person, then truly this person will not have lived in vain. There will be no room in us for any hope of a prompt death, because we will have a function to fulfill... "Let your light so shine before all, that seeing your good works they give glory to your Father, who is in heaven"⁵ (Matt. 5:16).

For pondering: Think of some of the flickers of light your departed loved one brought to the world. Share them with family and friends and thank God for each one of them.

---

5 *Death and Bereavement*. St. Stephen's Press. Oxford, England. 2002.

Two Empty Tombs

When I visited Jerusalem I saw two empty tombs. First, I knelt before the empty tomb of Jesus and prayed. Because His tomb is empty, my grave and your grave will one day be empty when He comes again to judge the living and the dead. "Christ is risen and the tombs are empty," sings St. John Chrysostom.

While still in Jerusalem I visited a second empty tomb, that of the Theotokos. The icon of the Dormition shows Jesus carrying her soul to heaven. The empty tomb of Jesus has already emptied the tomb of His mother just as it will empty your tomb and mine some day.

The icon of the Resurrection graphically expresses all this when it shows the Resurrected Lord, having destroyed the locks and gates of Hades, leading Adam and Eve, as well as all His faithful children, from the tomb to life eternal.

Christ's tomb is empty.

The tomb of the Theotokos is empty.

Your loved one's tomb is empty. "Why do you seek the living among the dead?" (Lk 24:5b)

Your tomb will one day be empty!

Why?

Because, "Christ is risen from the dead. By His death He has destroyed death and to those in the tombs He has bestowed life."

In the tender compassion of our God the dawn from on high shall break upon us, to shine on those who dwell in the darkness and the shadow of death and to guide our feet into the way of peace.

~ *Luke 1:78-79*

I shall change their mourning into gladness, comfort them, give them joy after their troubles.

~ *Jeremiah 31:13*

In Christ we have everything...
If you want to heal your wound, he is the doctor.
If you are burning with fever, he is the fountain.
If you are in need of help, he is strength.
If you are in dread of death, he is life.
If you are fleeing the darkness, he is light.
If you are hungry, he is food.
"O taste and see that the Lord is good! Blessed are they who take refuge in Him" (Ps. 34:8).

~ *Ambrose of Milan*

Replace "If Only" with "In Spite Of"

How often we suffer from those two little words, "if only."

If only I had a better job, a better education, a thinner waist, a bigger house, enough to retire on.

If only I hadn't started drinking, dropped out of school, quit that job, sold that stock, neglected my spouse.

How can we deal with those troublesome words? How many times St. Paul must have said, "If only I didn't have this thorn in the flesh, what great things I could do for the Lord." But soon St. Paul discovered that he was going to have to learn to live with that thorn. And he heard God say, "My grace is sufficient. For my power is made perfect in weakness."

That is our assurance, too. Whatever our limitations, we can be sure that there is a power greater than ourselves working through us: "My grace is sufficient."

Dr. Louis Pasteur had a stroke at age 46. He could have said, "if only" but he did not. Instead, he said "in spite of" and proceeded to lay the foundation for modern medicine through his discoveries.

There's Beethoven who became one of the world's greatest musicians after he experienced total deafness. He could have said "if only," but instead he said, "in spite of."

The trouble with "if only" is that it does not change anything. It keeps us facing the wrong direction; backward instead of forward. It is an expression of self pity, a way of feeling sorry for ourselves.

As we struggle through grief, God' grace will help us replace "if only" with "in spite of' and keep us looking forward.

Appetizers for Heaven

Joy will not have an end. The joyous experiences of life for us Christians serve as appetizers for heaven. Why does the sun feel so good? Why does that lake or mountain look so splendid? Why do birds and brooks make such beautiful music? Why is watermelon so refreshing on a hot summer day? What are all these pleasures and joys but appetizers for heaven.

God is trying to show us that if the pleasures and joys He provides for us on earth are so magnificent, how much greater are the blessings He has prepared for us and for our loved ones in heaven. In the words of Mother Teresa, "Never let anything so fill you with sorrow as to make you forget the joy of Christ risen."

Affliction comes to all,
not to make us sad, but sober;
not to make us sorry, but wise;
not to make us despondent, but its darkness to refresh us, as the
    night refreshes the day;
not to impoverish, but to enrich us, as the plow enriches the
    field;
to multiply our joy, as the seed, by planting, is multiplied a
    thousandfold.

~ H. Beecher

Grief is Like a Thunderstorm

Grief is foreboding like a dark cloudy day. There is darkness, thunder, lightning, searing winds. Torrents of rain begin to fall. Soon the clouds disperse. From behind the clouds, the sun's rays break out aiming majestic columns of light down toward earth. Then a beautiful rainbow arches across the sky.

How very much like grief. The dark clouds represent the inner grief. The thunder signifies the explosion of our emotions. The torrents of rain express the tears of mourning that pour out to unburden the heavy clouds of grief. Then, once this happens, the sun appears together with a rainbow to express the relief, comfort and peace that come once grief is released through mourning.

Such storms have a purpose. They represent the buildup of emotions. Once released, the skies of the earth as well as of the soul are cleansed and opened to see more clearly and to move steadily along the path of healing.

"Blessed are those who mourn for they shall be comforted." The soul would have no rainbow if the eyes had no tears.

St John Chrysostom described this phenomenon:

Anyone who prays in anguish will be able, after his prayer, to know a great joy in his soul. Just as clouds when they gather begin by making the day dark, then, once they have poured out all the water they contained, the atmosphere is serene and light, so anguish, as it builds up in our heart, plunges our thoughts into darkness, but then, when it has vented all its bitterness through prayer and accompanying tears, it brings to the soul a great light. God's influence irradiates the soul of the one who is praying, like a ray of sunlight.

Without "the resurrection of the dead and the life of the ages to come" (Nicene Creed), life would be as meaningless and as depressing as Eric Hoffer described it when he wrote, "We are condemned to death at birth, and life is a bus ride to the place of execution. All of our struggling and vying is about seats on the bus, and the ride is over before we know it."

"If Christ is not risen, our faith is futile and we are of all people most to be pitied," wrote St. Paul. So, we rejoice that life is not "a bus ride to the place of execution," but a journey from God to God, a journey to a place prepared especially for us by the risen Christ, Who said, "I go to prepare a place for you that where I am, you may be also."

Lord, let not the corrosive
fear of dying someday,
eat away the wonder of
living this day. Amen.

Fear of death and aging wipe out enjoying life today.

You have come to Mount Zion, the heavenly Jerusalem, the city of the living God. You have come to thousands upon thousands of angels in joyful assembly, to the church of the first-born, whose names are written in heaven.

~ Hebrews 12:22-23

Angels Meet Us at Death

We know from the words of Christ that the soul is met at death by angels. "And it came to pass that the beggar died, and that he was carried away by the angels into Abraham's bosom" (Luke 16:22 RSV).

In this parable Jesus is telling us that Lazarus the beggar who died was not escorted but "carried by the angels" to God. What an experience it must have been for the lifelong beggar living on crumbs suddenly to find himself carried by the angels to God.

I've heard someone describe having watched Queen Elizabeth returning to Buckingham Palace from an overseas trip. There is the parade of dignitaries, the marching bands, the formations of splendor, and the fanfare that accompanies royalty. Yet nothing – absolutely nothing – can compare with the home going of a true Christian who says goodbye to all of the suffering, the difficulties and the problems of this life, and then is surrounded immediately by angels and carried by them to a glorious welcome in heaven.

One medical doctor who has studied people who were dying relates this experience:

> *He was sedated, fully conscious, and had a low temperature. He was a rather religious person who believed in life after death. We expected him to die, and he probably did too, as he was asking us to pray for him. In the room where he was lying, there was a staircase leading to the second*

floor. Suddenly he exclaimed: 'See, the angels are coming down the stairs. The glass has fallen and broken.' All of us in the room looked toward the staircase where a drinking glass had been placed on one of the steps. As we looked, we saw the glass break into a thousand pieces without any apparent cause. It did not fall; it simply exploded. The angels, of course, we did not see. A happy and peaceful expression remained on his face.

Another doctor relates this experience:

The condition of the man suffering from a heart attack had been serious for the last few days. Suddenly he gained consciousness. He looked better and cheerful. He talked nicely to his relatives and requested them to go home. He also said, "I shall go to my home. Angels have come to take me away." He looked relieved and cheerful.

Give rest with the saints, O Christ, to the soul of your servant, in a place where there is no pain, no sorrow, no suffering, but life everlasting.

~ Orthodox Funeral Service

Precious in the sight of the Lord is the death of His faithful ones.

~ Psalm 116:15

Angels Will be There to Help Us

Death is the biggest crisis we will ever face. That is the time when we need help the most, and the angels will be there to help us! St. John Chrysostom wrote that he knew that "when Christians are about to pass away, if they happen to have received the Mysteries (Holy Communion) with a pure conscience just before they breath their last, a bodyguard of angels escorts them away for the sake of what they have received," i.e., the precious Body and Blood of Christ.

It is for this reason that we believe that death can be beautiful. People have died with wonderful expressions of joy on their faces. It is no wonder that David said, "Even though I walk through the valley of the shadow of death, I fear no evil" (Ps. 23:4).

Be Steadfast

There are many dying people who live in dreadful fear of death. They may be suffering greatly but because of Christ, who by His death has destroyed death for us, we now have the promise that in a moment they will be transformed. The glories, beauties, splendor and grandeur of heaven will soon be theirs. They will be surrounded by heavenly messengers sent by God to carry them home to a place where "eye has not seen, ear has not heard, nor has it ever entered into the heart of man what things God has prepared for those who love Him." That is why St. Paul tells us in his great resurrection chapter, 1 Corinthians 15, "Therefore my beloved brethren, be steadfast, immovable, always abounding in the work of the Lord, knowing that in the Lord your labor is not in vain" (1 Cor. 15:58).

An oncologist, professor at a large U.S. medical school, relates that she sat with a family beside their seven-year-old girl who was in the last stages of leukemia. "She had the final energy to sit up and say, 'The angels – they're so beautiful! Mommy, can you see them? Do you hear their singing? I've never heard such beautiful singing!'" Then the child died. The doctor continued, "The word that most closely describes what I felt is 'gift.' It wasn't just that the child was given the gift of peace in the moment of pain, but that this was a gift to her parents. And it was a gift to me as her doctor. I felt privileged to be there."

Such visions are good but we cannot consider them as proof of the hereafter. Such assurance comes to us only from the word of God. It is not because of such visions that we believe in the afterlife, but because of our Lord's resurrection. Such visions, however, may be considered as part of the grace of God which constantly seeks to nudge us into belief. It is a beautiful "bonus."

Present with Us in Every Liturgy

In the stupendous vision of Isaiah, the throne of God is surrounded by angels – the seraphim and the cherubim – prostrating themselves before God and offering a sevenfold doxology of praise and adoration.

But there before God's throne stand not only the angels but all the redeemed of God; all the saints of God – "saints" not because they were sinless but because they have been washed in the blood of the Lamb. All those who repented and kept receiving the precious Body and Blood of Jesus "for the forgiveness of sins and unto life eternal" – they will all be there before the throne of God with their white baptismal robes.

Thus, together with the angels, surrounding the throne of God, are the saints of all ages – all of God's Holy, Catholic, Apostolic Church. Adam is there. Eve, Abel, Abraham, Isaac, Jacob, Daniel, Peter, Paul, Barnabas. And take heart, you who mourn and see but dimly through the tears. Your beloved husband or wife is there. A brother perhaps or a sister, mother and father long since deceased. All are there. And best of all, Jesus is there. He is the Lamb of God who takes away the sins of the world. Before His throne the angels and the saints all together give Him praise and honor and glory night and day. All our departed loved ones, for example, are present also before God's earthly throne when we celebrate the liturgy. The church triumphant in heaven and the church militant on earth are present in every liturgy. This is why we remember the dead in each liturgy – because they are indeed with us. They are not dead but living and are with us before the throne of God. Together with

them and all the angels we offer glory, praise and honor to the
Triune God, Father, Son and Holy Spirit.

The cry of man's anguish went up to God,
    "Lord take away the pain;
The shadow that darkens the world Thou hast made,
    The close-coiling chain
That strangles the heart, the burden that weighs
    On the wings that would soar,
Lord, take away pain from the world Thou hast made,
    That it love Thee the more."
Then answered the Lord to the cry of His world:
    "Shall I take away pain,
And with it the power of the soul to endure,
    Made strong by the strain?
Shall I take away pity, that knits heart to heart
    And sacrifice high?
Will ye lose all your heroes that lift from the fire
    White brows to the sky?
Shall I take away love that redeems with a price
    And smiles at its loss?
Can ye spare from your lives that would climb unto Me
    the Christ on His cross?"

The Joy of Heaven

Anthony DeStefano has written a delightful book entitled *A Travel Guide to Heaven*.[6] He writes that when most people think of heaven, they miss completely one key ingredient: fun. He writes,

You see, if heaven is anything at all, it's fun. It is a place of unlimited pleasure, unlimited happiness, and unlimited joy. Think about that for a second and consider what an incredibly outrageous concept it is. That's why it's so surprising that while an overwhelming majority of the general public believes in heaven, not many people seem to be bubbling over with excitement about it. In fact, not many people seem to be thinking about it at all.

This is partly because heaven is so hard for us to understand. With all the problems and suffering that constantly envelop our lives, it's difficult to grasp the reality of paradise, a place where there is no pain, no evil, no disappointment, no death.

Another reason is simply that we've heard so much about heaven since our childhoods that the whole idea has gotten a bit stale. Familiarity hasn't exactly bred contempt, but it has bred boredom...C.S. Lewis said, that "the serious business of heaven is joy."

Your departed loved one is now experiencing that joy.

---

6 Doubleday. New York, N.Y. 2003.

God is Faithful in Our Dark Nights

Grief is a passion to endure. People can be stricken with it, victims of it, stuck in it.

Or they can meet it, get through it, and become quiet victors through the active, honest, and courageous process of grieving.

~ *A. Bozarth, Ph.D.*

A person who had suffered greatly wrote, "I found God faithful in my grief; I found Jesus real; I tasted the resurrection glory; I found a supportive fellowship in family and friends; I found that for me Jesus is life and love!

In order to pass from the slavery of Egypt to the Promised Land, one has to pass through the desert. Likewise, one has to pass through the desert of the dry moments of life, what has been called "the dark night of the soul". This is the cross. And there is no other way to heaven (the promised land) than the cross.

It is good for us at times to have troubles and adversities; for often they make a man enter into himself, so that he may know that he is in exile, and may not place his hopes in anything of this world.

~ *Thomas à Kempis*

Not an End but a Beginning

Metropolitan Anthony of Sourozh said,

St Paul could say: "For me to live is Christ." Death will be a gain, because as long as I live in this body I am separated from Christ. This is why he said in another passage that for him to die is not to divest himself of this temporary life: for him, to die means to be clothed in eternity. It is not an end; it is a beginning. It is a door that opens and allows us into the vastness of eternity which would be closed for us forever if death did not free us from our integration into earthly things.

In our attitude to death these two aspects must each play a role. When a person dies we can legitimately be heartbroken. We can look with horror at the fact that sin has murdered a person whom we love. We can deny the fact that we accept death as the last word, the last event in life. We are right when we weep over the departed, because this should not be. He or she was killed by evil. On the other hand we can rejoice for the person who has died because new life, unbounded, free, has begun for him or her. And again, we can weep for ourselves, our bereavement, our loneliness, but at the same time we must learn that... love... does not allow the memory of the beloved to fade, the love that makes us speak of our relationship with the beloved one not in the past tense: "I loved him, we were so close," but makes us think in the present tense: "I love her; we are so close."[7]

---

7 *Death and Bereavement*. St. Stephen's Press. Oxford, England. 2002.

Our Trials Teach Us

God sometimes shuts the door
    and shuts us in,
That He may speak, perchance
    through grief and pain,
and softly, heart to heart,
    above the din,
May tell some precious
    thought to us again.

The one who fears to be alone will never be anything but lonely, no matter how much he may surround himself with people. But the one who learns, in solitude and recollection, to be at peace with his own loneliness, and to prefer its reality to the illusion of merely natural companionship, comes to know the invisible companionship of God.

~ Thomas Merton

Man withers like a flower and passes like a dream and every man comes to end. And when the trumpet will sound again the dead will rise like in a quake to greet you, O Christ God. At that time, grant, O Lord, that the one You have taken from us, the soul of Your servant, be in fellowship with Your saints.

~ Orthodox Funeral Service

Goodbye for Now, Dear

The evenings were always a pleasant time of day, when my wife and I would sit side by side, in our easy chairs, to spend a relaxing evening. It wouldn't be long when out of the corner of my eye, I would notice her head nodding and she would fall off to sleep. It was then that I would turn my head and look fully at that beautiful face. I would allow my mind to wander back over the past fifty years and think of all the things we shared. The love and the heartaches, the happy times and the sickness, the ventures and the failures – yet our love and respect always prevailed.

There is nowhere we would rather be than in our chairs sharing these precious quiet moments.

Her chair is empty now but those years of beautiful memories help in some way.

How lucky I have been to be so privileged. Goodbye for now, dear.

~ Ted Roberts

Prayer is giving my sorrows and fears to God and receiving His peace in return.

~ Philippians 4:6-7, paraphrased

The void, emptiness, sorrow and pain you feel inside will one day subside.

The laughter, joy and happy times, will once again shine.

Life is full of obstacles, some are higher to climb, but with faith and patience anything can be overcome, in time.

~ L. Wynkoop

Trusting God No Matter What

After Job's misery accomplished its purpose, God stopped the pain and replaced it with bounty. Job's wealth was double what it had been before. Even Job's family doubled: Job's ten children in heaven were matched by another ten on earth. This shows that although God may let us endure hardship at times, the Lord does love to bless his people. The God who sometimes takes away is also the God who gives and keeps on giving. In the end God will wipe every tear away and give eternal, unbroken happiness to all who love Him. In the meantime we must trust God no matter what.

I'll lend you for a little time a child of mine, He said.
For you to love while he lives,
and mourn when he is dead.
It may be six or seven years, or twenty-two or three.
But will you, till I call him back, take care of him for me?
He'll bring his charms to gladden you,
and shall his stay be brief,
You'll have his lovely memories as solace for your grief.
I cannot promise he will stay, since all from earth return,
But there are lessons taught down there
I want this child to learn.
I've looked the wide world over
in my search for teachers true
And from the throngs that crowd life's lanes,
I have selected you.
Now will you give him all your love,
nor think the labor vain,
Nor hate me when I come to call, to take him back again?
I fancied that I heard them say, Dear Lord,
Thy will he done. For all the joy
Thy child shall bring, the risk of grief we'll run.
We'll shelter him with tenderness,
we'll love him while we may;
And for the happiness we've known,
will ever grateful stay.
But shall the angels call for him
much sooner than we planned,
We'll brave the bitter grief that comes,
and try to understand.

~ Edgar Guest

The Difference Between Grieving and Mourning

Grief and mourning are not the same. Grief consists of the interior thoughts and feelings that we experience after the loss of a loved one. Mourning, on the other hand, is when the interior feelings of sorrow are expressed outwardly. As someone said mourning is "grief gone public." We express our inner grief by crying and talking about the person who died. Keeping grief bottled up inside can cause depression and even physical ailments. Blessed is the person who has a caring family and friends to whom to ventilate outwardly this inner grief. Such a person is on the way to recovery.

An example of such outward sharing of one's inner grief is exemplified in the following story by S. Kidd,

It was 6:00 PM, and I sat in the shadows of my bedroom, tears glazing my eyes. Recently some painful memories had surfaced in my life. I'd offered them to God, but the aching hadn't stopped yet. Healing, I knew, took time, and tears were part of the process. They made wet splotches on my blouse. That's how my husband Sandy found me when he arrived home from work. He didn't say a word. But in what is surely one of the most precious moments of our marriage, he touched his finger to the tears winding down my face, then touched his wet finger to his own cheek. His gesture went straight to my heart, saying more than words ever could. Your tears run down my face, too. I share your pain. I am with you. Inexplicably, my sadness lightened, as if he had taken half of it into himself. That day I learned what a deep and beautiful gift it is to share another person's suffering, simply to be there, willing to blend my tears with theirs.

Jesus did not say, "Blessed are those who *grieve...*" Those who internalize their grief and do not express it through tears and mourning find no release as do those who express it through mourning. This is why Jesus said, "Blessed are those who *mourn*, for they shall be comforted." Mourning is the external expression of inner grief.

Why do people die horrible deaths with cancer, heart disease, etc.? Why do natural disasters take the lives of people without distinction to their morality or status in life? Why doesn't God answer our prayers? We don't know. We can say that God has a purpose in mind too big for us to understand. But even that doesn't help us too much. What we can hold on to is the fact that Jesus is the Resurrection and that He will bring back to life all those who fall asleep in Him. No matter how long the world will last or how long my name may have been forgotten, Christ will remember and will raise me to life. You and I matter to Him eternally.

Sleep (or Lack Thereof)

Like most widows and widowers, 1 had trouble getting to sleep at night. Being alone in our king-sized bed emphasized the terrible loneliness that assailed me at night. In order to ignore that loneliness, I would plan my next day's activities. That was no solution. There were so many items on that list in my head that I couldn't relax. Here are a few remedies that worked for me.

- Cut back on drinks with caffeine.
- Exercise daily.
- Keep a book handy and read until your eyelids grow heavy.
- Have a cup of herbal tea to relax tired muscles and an active mind.
- Try a hot, soaking bath to relax muscles.
- Take time to unwind before going to bed: watch TV (not a horror show), read, meditate or pray.
- Write thoughts, hopes and dreams in a journal.
- Write down a list of things to do the next day. (This keeps them from running around in your head).

If at all possible, stay away from sleeping pills. The National Academy of Science's Institute of Medicine says that these medicines have a cumulative effect. If you take them for a week, there is four to six times more in your bloodstream on day seven than there was on day one. Be sure to consult your doctor about any long-term use.

~ *C. Curry*

An ancient rabbi said, "When a man suffers, he ought not to say: 'That's bad! That's bad!' Nothing that God imposes on man is bad. But it is all right to say: 'That's bitter!' For among medicines there are some that are made with bitter herbs." To those who love God, suffering may be bitter but not bad.

Rejoice that God loves us that much. Be glad that He wants us to be a little breathless for heaven. Be thankful that He never wastes any of our experiences.

"Don't be surprised, dear friends, at the painful trials you are suffering, as though something strange were happening to you. But rejoice that you participate in Christ's suffering, so that you may be overjoyed when His glory is revealed." So wrote Peter to first-century Christians (1 Pet. 4:12,13), and it applies to us today.

The most common physical symptom of deep grief is low energy. You may need a lot of extra sleep. Be sure to allow for it. Sleep is more than just escape. Your body needs more rest, just as your soul does, and you may need the necessary dream time of extra sleep.

~ *A.R. Bozarth*

Exercise

The importance of daily exercise for the newly widowed cannot be overemphasized, even though the last thing we want to do is add more physical activities to our daily routine. Scientific studies show that regular exercise stimulates chemicals in the brain which in turn eliminate depression, making us happier and more alert. The American Medical Association recommends three 20-minute sessions of vigorous activity weekly. In addition to the usual suggestions of walking, running, swimming, tennis and bicycling, they include garden work in their list. For many people, gardening is more than exercise; it is a labor of love that helps them slow down and reduce tension in their lives.

~ *C. Curry*

Why Some People Will Avoid You

Don't be surprised if old friends begin to shy away from one who has lost a loved one. Your presence will be a constant reminder of death to them. They will feel uncomfortable in your presence and will seek to avoid you. This will cause you sorrow, but try to understand. Seek out people close to you who are willing to listen. Tell them how you feel and what you need.

Finding Meaning in Grief

Our grief work is never really complete until we have found meaning in our loss. It is not just our emotions that need healing, so does our theology, our belief system.

Clare Boothe Luce, a noted author, said once, "Grief has a great purgative value. Since God cannot fill the soul until it is emptied of all trivial concerns, a great grief is a tremendous bonfire, in which all the trash of life is burned."

Dr. Viktor E. Frankl was the founder of logotherapy, a psychiatric approach that believes that in order to survive and move on in life people need to find meaning in what happens to them. He tells the following story:

Once, an elderly general practitioner consulted me because of his severe depression. He could not overcome the loss of his wife who had died two years before and whom he had loved above all else. Now how could I help him? What should I tell him? Well, I refrained from telling him anything but instead confronted him with the question, "What would have happened, Doctor, if you had died first and your wife would have had to survive you?" "Oh," he said, "for her this would have been terrible; how she would have suffered!" Whereupon I replied, "You see, Doctor, such a suffering has been spared her, and it was you who have spared her this suffering; but now, you have to pay for it by surviving and mourning her." He said no word but shook my hand and calmly left my office. Suffering ceases to be suffering in some way at the moment it finds meaning.

Another person whose wife died after 57 years of marriage was depressed to the point of suicide. "But one thing saved me," he said. "It was a remark that my daughter made to me. Perhaps seeing the depressed state I was in, and speaking for her brother as well, she said, 'Dad, you have lost a wife. But we have lost a mother, and you are the only one left to us, and we need you.' Until then I had not realized that I was not alone in my grief. They felt it as strongly as I did, and I did not realize how important or how necessary I was to them. It gave me the incentive to live and perhaps even to weather this thing out."

"You are the only one left, and we need you." Think of the persons in your family who need you in the same way. Try to be there for them.

The pain we suffer as we watch a loved one die is like the pain of childbirth: our loved one is about to be born into a new life.

What We Had Was a Gift

Much of the sorrow we experience in death would not be possible if God had not been so good to us. Job realized this when he said, "The Lord gave and the Lord has taken away. Blessed be the name of the Lord" (Job 1:21). When grieving, most of us focus on the words, "the Lord has taken away." We forget the first part of the verse, "the Lord gave." Indeed, He is the One who gave us that dear person who died. He did not take away anyone that He didn't give us in the first place. So, even as we grieve the passing of a loved one, we need to give thanks for what God gave us to enjoy for a while. What we had was a gift from God, not something we had earned.

A certain person who lost his wife, his daughter and his mother in a terrible auto accident wrote, "I did not deserve to lose three members of my family. But, then again, I am not sure I deserved to have them in the first place. I did not deserve their deaths, but I did not deserve their presence in my life either."

Thus, when we grieve and mourn the loss of a loved one, may we remember at the same time how much God has given us. Truly, "The Lord gave and the Lord has taken away. Blessed be the name of the Lord" (Job 1:21).

Jesus Christ is no security against storms, but He is perfect security in storms. He has never promised you an easy passage, only a safe landing.

In this sad world of ours,
        sorrow comes to all...
Perfect relief is not possible,
        except with time.
You cannot now realize
        that you will ever feel better...
And yet this is a mistake.
        You are sure
to be happy again.

~ *Abraham Lincoln*

Life is the childhood of our immortality.

~ *Goethe*

Indeed the mystery of death is awesome! How the soul is suddenly separated from the body! And how the natural bond of being together is cut off by the divine will! So we pray to you: O Lifegiver and Lover of man, give rest to the one departed this life in the company of the just.

~ *Orthodox Funeral Service*

Refusing to Face Reality

One of the striking characteristics of our time is the absurd lengths to which we go to keep death out of sight and out of mind. Dr. John Brantner, a University of Minnesota clinical psychologist, said that American society "deals very badly with death and the dying... As a society we fear death and through our fear we foster it." Studies have shown that dying patients want very much to talk about death. It helps them accept it and relieves anxiety, but few people are comfortable about bringing up the subject.

Tolstoy, in his masterful tale *The Death of Ivan Ilyitch* describes the conspiracy of silence that we maintain in the presence of the dying. "Ivan Ilyitch's chief torment was a lie – the lie somehow accepted by everyone that he was only sick, but not dying and that he needed only to be calm."

Simone de Beauvoir, in *A Very Easy Death*, writes of her mother dying of cancer, "At the time the truth was crushing her, and when she needed to escape it by talking, we were condemning her to silence, we forced her to say nothing about the anxieties and to suppress her doubts, she felt both guilty and misunderstood."

In earlier days, along with the other basic facts of life like birth, marriage, bearing children, and raising a family, death was openly accepted as a fact of life. The burial ground surrounding the church stood in the very center of the community. The body was not viewed in a funeral parlor; it was brought right into the living room of one's home. One could not evade the fact of death. One had to accept it and learn to live with it.

Through Christ, with Christ (1 Thess. 4:14) and in Christ (1 Cor. 15:22), through the power of the Spirit (Rom 8:11), God will bestow life upon the dead and raise their bodies. He will heal them from every ill, according to the word He spoke to the Prophet Isaiah: "Thy dead shall live, their bodies shall rise. O dwellers in the dust, awake and sing for joy!" (Isa. 26:19). The body will be delivered from its former infirmities and will recover its original integrity.[8]

~ Jean-Claude Larchet

Disappointments can often be His appointments. through them God often points to a better way.

As the mountains are round about Jerusalem, so the Lord is round about His people, from this time forth and forevermore.

~ Psalm 125:2

---

8 *"The Theology of Illness,"* SVS Press. 2002.

Our Church Calendar

Our Church calendar provides many occasions when we are asked to face up to the fact of death. Good Friday is one such occasion. So is Easter. Sunday is another. Every Sunday is a "little Easter" celebrating Christ's victory over death. On our Church calendar every year, there are special Memorial Saturdays or "Saturdays of the Souls" which provide another opportunity for us to face up to death, i.e., the three Saturdays preceding Great Lent and the Saturday before Pentecost. On these Saturdays, the Divine Liturgy is celebrated and special prayers are offered for our deceased loved ones. We pray for the dead especially on Saturdays since it was on the Sabbath day that Christ lay dead in the tomb, "resting from all His works and trampling down death by death." Thus, in the New Testament, Saturday becomes the proper day for remembering the dead and offering prayers for them.

Time does not heal. Prayer heals. The Holy Spirit heals. Relinquish your loved one to God who heals.

Bereavement was a learning experience when I opened my heart and let God in. The question is "Do I want to spend the rest of my life grieving, mourning the loss of my love, and feeling sorry for myself, or do I want to move through the pain, close the door gently on the past, learn to enjoy the present moment and look forward to the future?"

~ *C. Curry*

Why should you weep? For Jesus rose from the dead; so shall you. Be of good cheer and confidence. You are not lost when you are put into the tomb; you are but seed sown to ripen against the eternal harvest. Your spirit mounts to God; your body slumbers for a while to be quickened into eternal life; it cannot be quickened except it die; but when it dies, it shall receive a new life; it shall not be destroyed.

~ *C. Spurgeon*

Focus on Ourselves

Whether our prayers for our departed loved ones bring any benefit to them we know not; we leave this to the mercy of God. But of one thing we are certain; such prayers do benefit those who pray for the departed. They remind us that we too are going to die; they strengthen faith in the life beyond; they nourish reverence toward those who have died; they help build hope in divine mercy; they develop brotherly love among those who survive. They make us more cautious and diligent in getting ready for that ultimate journey which will unite us with our departed loved ones and usher us into the presence of God. They remind us that now is the time for moral development and improvement, for faith, repentance and love; now is the time to strive for the crown of righteousness which the Lord, the righteous Judge, will award to those "who have fought the good fight, finished the race and kept the faith" (2 Tim. 4:7).

Archbishop William Temple said once, "We do not pray for them because God will otherwise neglect them. We pray for them because we know that He loves and cares for them, and we claim the privilege of uniting our love for them with God's." Not to pray for them would be tantamount to believing that they do not exist anymore. In Father Makary's words, "We are all alive in Him, for in Him there is no death."

A physician was visiting a patient who knew that he was dying, and asked to be comforted about the next life. The physician was a Christian, but he wasn't accustomed to lecturing on immortality, and he sat wondering where to begin. At that moment his dog was heard scratching at the door; it had escaped from the car, and had sniffed out where its master was. The physician let the dog in and then drew the moral. The dog had never been in this room before: it knew only that its master was there, and that was enough: it wanted to be with him. Our road will bring us through unknown passages to a door we can't open: but if we know that on the other side of it is Jesus, and that He will let us in, that's enough.

~ J.R. MacPhail

Why Do We Pray for the Dead? (Part 1)

Christianity is a religion of love. Praying for the dead is an expression of love. We ask God to remember our departed because we love them. Love relationships survive death and even transcend it. There is an inner need for a relationship with a loved one to continue to be expressed even after a loved one has died. Often even more so after a loved one has died since physical communication is no longer possible. The Church encourages us to express our love for our departed brethren through memorial services and prayers.

The anniversary of the death of a loved one is very painful. The Church helps us cope with this pain by encouraging us to have memorial prayers offered in church for departed loved ones on the anniversaries of their deaths (forty days after the death, six months, a year, etc.) This gives us the opportunity to do something for our loved one. It helps express our love and resolve our grief.

A little boy sat quietly in a train traveling to one of the coast cities of our country on an especially hot day. The countryside was quite interesting. The little fellow sat patiently watching the row on row of cultivated cornfields and wooded pastures go by. Finally a motherly old lady leaned forward and asked sympathetically, "Little boy, aren't you tired of this long hot ride?" The lad looked up brightly and replied with a smile, "Yes, Ma'am, a little, but I don't mind it much because my father is going to meet me when I get to the city."

So we too can anticipate that God will be there to meet us at our final destination. Indescribable joy waits there for all who love Him.

"Take my yoke upon you... For my yoke is easy and my burden is light" (Matt. 11:29-30). A yoke is built for two: you on one side, and Jesus on the other. The result is a lighter burden.

An essential for healing is to release regrets. What you did or did not do; did or did not say. Part of the healing is to forgive yourself. And the other.

Why Do We Pray for the Dead? (Part 2)

Death may take loved ones out of sight but it certainly does not take them out of mind, or out of heart. We continue to love them and think of them as we believe they continue to love us and think of us. How can a mother forget a child who has passed over to the life beyond? The same love which led her to pray for that child when he lived will guide her to pray for him now. For in Christ all are living. The same love makes her wish to communicate with him. Yet, all communication must take place in Christ and through Christ. No other communication with the dead is possible or lawful for the Christian. God is God of the living. Our dear ones live in Him. Only through Him is it possible for us to communicate with them. Every liturgy in the Orthodox Church contains prayers for the dead such as the following: "Be mindful also of all those who slumber in the hope of a resurrection to everlasting life. Give them rest, O God, where the light of Thy countenance shineth."

Just as we pray for the deceased, so we believe they continue to love us, remember us, and pray for us now that they are closer to God. We cannot forget the example of the rich man in Hades asking Abraham to send Lazarus to warn his brothers lest they, too, go to that place of torment. Though he had left this life, he did not cease to be concerned for his brothers still on earth.

The Orthodox Church prays for the dead to express her faith that all who have fallen asleep in the Lord, live in the Lord; their lives are hidden with Christ in God (Col. 3:3).

Whether on earth or in heaven, the Church is a single family, one Body in Christ. Death changes the location but it cannot sever the bond of love.

In the old days, death was always one of the party. Now he sits next to me at the dinner table: I have to make friends with him. Do not seek death. Death will find you. But seek the road that makes death a fulfillment.

~ *Dag Hammarskjold*

Where is the desire of the world? Where is the pomp of the temporal? Where are the gold and the silver? Where is all the gathering and noise of friends? All is dust, all is ashes, all is shadow. But let us come to pray to the Immortal King: O Lord, deem the one departed from us worthy of your eternal blessing and give him rest in the everlasting happiness of heaven.

~ *Orthodox Funeral Service*

What Can We Expect of our Prayers for the Dead?

Since a person's eternal destiny is determined immediately after death (though one must wait for the General Judgment to receive the full measure of one's reward), we must not expect our prayers to snatch an unbeliever from Hades to Paradise. It is our present life that determines our eternal destiny. Now is the time to repent and accept God's grace. Death puts an end to that state and commits each person to his special judgment. This is why the Lord said that work must be done, "while it is day" because "the night cometh when no man can work" (John 9:4). "Day" means the present life, "when it is still possible to believe," writes St. Chrysostom, while "night" is the condition after death.

What happens beyond the grave belongs entirely to God. He has told us as much as we need to know; the rest is covered with a veil of mystery which man's curiosity is incapable of piercing. The faithful have committed themselves to God for the duration of their earthly lives. Now, it is well and good for them to commit their departed loved ones to the mercy of God through prayer, for they have the assurance that God in the riches of His mercy has ways to help them beyond our knowing. Some church fathers believe that our departed loved ones experience a kind of spiritual relief as a result of the prayers of their loved ones on earth.

The grave has lost its terror. As I go toward heaven I can shout, "O death! Where is thy sting?" and I hear the answer falling down from Calvary – "Buried in the bosom of the Son of God." He took the sting right out of death for me, and received it into his own bosom. Take a hornet and pluck the sting out; you are not afraid of it after that, any more than of a fly. So death has lost its sting. What a glorious thought that when you die you but sink into the arms of Jesus, to be borne to the land of everlasting rest! "To die," the apostle says, "is gain."

~ *D. Moody*

I could never myself believe in God, if it were not for the cross. The only God I believe in is the one Nietzsche ridiculed as "God on the Cross." In the real world of pain, how could one worship a God who was immune to it! I have entered many Buddhist temples and stood respectfully before the statue of Buddha, his legs crossed, arms folded, eyes closed, the ghost of a smile playing round his mouth, a remote look on his face, detached from the agonies of the world. But each time after a while I have had to turn away. And in imagination I have turned instead to that lonely, twisted, tortured figure on the cross, nails through hands and feet, back lacerated, limbs wrenched, brow bleeding from thorn-pricks, mouth dry and intolerably thirsty, plunged in God-forsaken darkness. That is the God for me! He laid aside his immunity to pain. He entered our world of flesh and blood, tears and death. He suffered for us.

~ *John Stott*

A Meaningful Custom

It is customary among Orthodox Christians from Greece to bring a tray of boiled wheat kernels to church for the memorial service. The wheat kernels express belief in everlasting life. Jesus said, "'Unless a grain of wheat falls into the earth and dies, it remains alone, but if it dies, it bears much fruit" (John 12:24). Just as new life rises from the buried kernel of wheat, so we believe the one buried will rise one day to a new life with God. The wheat kernels are covered with sugar and raisins to express the bliss of eternal life with God in heaven. St. Paul writes, "So it is with the resurrection of the dead. What is sown is perishable, what is raised is imperishable. It is sown in dishonor, it is raised in glory. It is sown in weakness, it is raised in power. It is sown a physical body, it is raised a spiritual body" (1 Cor. 15:42-44).

Memorial prayer services which affirm the reality of physical death and also the reality of resurrection into life eternal play a vital role in the healing of grief for the Orthodox Christian.

The names of the departed are remembered in prayer in every liturgy. Names may be given to the priest weekly – if desired – not only of the dead but also of the living. The list of names should be submitted in two columns: one list marked *Living in the Lord* and one marked *Asleep in the Lord*. The list may be mailed or given to the priest before liturgy.

Death is the invitation God gives us to go farther on, where there is still a greater beauty to behold, still deeper mystery to be solved, still greater fellowship to be enjoyed, a still greater height to climb.

Death is an invitation to go farther on.

Many a time, having lifted myself on an X-ray table,
I have heard the nurse intone,
"Don't move, don't breathe."
Then after an endless moment,
"You may breathe."
Someday when I lie dying, a voice will whisper to me,
"Don't move, don't breathe."
And in that breathless interim,
I will cross to the beyond and hear God saying,
"You may breathe."

~ *E. Rothchild*

There is a Russian lady in the Orthodox community at Oxford who strongly objects to being called a widow. Although her husband died many years ago, she insists: "I am his wife, not his widow." She is right.

~ *Bishop Kallistos Ware*

Love Never Forgets

Dr. Paul Tillich believed that the anxiety of having to die is the anxiety that one will be forgotten both now and in eternity. Burial means a removal from the face of the earth. This is what we cannot endure. Memorial markers will not keep us from being forgotten. One day they will crumble to dust. The only thing that can keep us from being forgotten is our faith that God knew us before we were born and will remember us for all eternity.

In a lesser but still very real way, memorial prayers offered by loved ones serve to relieve the anxiety of being forgotten.

The first child of Dr. Martineau, an eminent minister, died in infancy and was buried in the French cemetery of Dublin. Before they left Ireland for Liverpool, the father and mother paid a farewell visit to the grave of their first-born son. The years went by. Mrs. Martineau died. At the age of 87, Dr. Martineau was a lonely old man. But when he was at the tercentenary of Dublin University, he stole away from the brilliant public function to stand once more by the tiny grave that held the dust of his firstborn child. No other living soul recalled that little one's smile or remembered where the child was sleeping. But the father knew and the little buried hands held his heart. A father's heart never forgets. Love always remembers. That is why the Orthodox Church has always encouraged us to sponsor special memorial prayers and services for the departed.

Phillips Brooks wrote to a friend whose wife had died suddenly.

"She is not dead, but living," said Phillips Brooks, "and if you are sure that God's love is holding her and educating her, you can be very contentedly with her in spirit and look forward confidently to the day when you shall also go to God and be with her.

"I know this does not take away your pain – no one can do that, not even God – but it can help you to bear it, to be brave and cheerful, to do your duty, and to live the pure, earnest, spiritual life which she in heaven wishes you to live. It is the last effort of unselfishness, the last token which you can give her of the love you bear her, that you let her pass out of your sight to go to God... My dear friend, she is yours forever. God never takes away what He has once given."

O God of spirits and of all flesh, who overcame death and vanquished the devil and gave life to your world, the same Lord, give rest to the soul of Your departed servant (N.) in a place of light, in a place of happiness, in a place of peace, where there is no pain, sorrow or suffering.

Gracious and merciful God, forgive every sin committed by him, whether by word, deed or thought. For there is no man who lives and does not sin. You alone are without sin. Your righteousness is righteousness forever and Your word is truth.

~ *Orthodox Funeral Service*

Dealing with Anger

Many people get angry when they lose a loved one. They may feel angry at the one who left. They may even feel angry toward God. These feelings are normal. Even devout persons experience feelings of anger toward God. Some feelings become harmful to us if we are unable to admit them to ourselves and God. If we do not deal with these feelings, they will take over and consume us.

One outlet for anger is prayer. Prayer is conversation or dialogue with the best Friend we have, Jesus. There is nothing wrong with expressing angry feelings to Jesus. If anyone understands, He does. David in his Psalms, which are classic examples of prayer, often expresses angry feelings to God. He even complains about the way God treats him.

Another healthy outlet for anger is the Sacrament of Confession. Sit down with your spiritual father and express these feelings to him, then kneel before the icon of Christ and confess them to Jesus for His forgiveness. In addition to these outlets, psychologists suggest sports, long brisk walks, push-ups, golf, tennis and bowling as excellent releases for anger and hostility.

Oh! Think not that the worm has eaten up your children, your friends, your husband, your father, your aged parents – true the worms seem to have devoured them. Oh! What is the worm after all but the filter through which our poor filthy flesh must go? For in the twinkling of an eye at the last trumpet we shall be raised incorruptible, and the living shall be changed; you shall see the eye that just now has been closed, and you shall look on it again; you shall again grasp the hand that just now fell motionless at the side; you shall kiss the lips that just now were clay-cold and white, and you shall hear again the voice that is silent in the tomb. They shall live again. And you that fear death – why fear to die? Jesus died before you, and He passed through the iron gates, and as He passed them before you, He will come and meet you. Jesus who lives can make the dying bed feel soft as downy pillows are.

~ *C. Spurgeon*

There will be no despondency in heaven – for "God shall wipe away all tears from their eyes; and there shall be no more death, neither sorrow, nor crying, neither shall there be any more pain: for the former things are passed away."

~ *Revelations 21:4*

A Parade of Memories

A psychotherapist once said that what people who have lost a loved one need is a parade. He meant a parade of memories. Such a parade is a joyful way of letting the happy memories of a loved one take the place of the pain of loss.

It is said that God gave us memory so that we might have roses in winter. Recalling and savoring the happy memories of a loved one can bring great consolation in the winter of our grief.

Make it a point to talk about the deceased with your family and friends. Recall the beautiful memories. Savor them. Enjoy them. Praise God for them. Recall them as often as you wish. A happy memory never wears out. It brings continual healing.

After Dr. Elizabeth Kubler-Ross theorized that acceptance of death was the final stage in our grief process, several self-help groups sprang up to help terminally ill patients attain that final stage. Yet, did Jesus accept his own death calmly? When we look at the account of how He faced death in the Garden of Gethsemane, we fail to see a scene of calm acceptance. To the contrary, we see Him sweating drops of blood and begging His Father for some other way. For Jesus, death was not to be accepted. It was the "last enemy" (1 Cor. 15:26) that needed to be destroyed – which He did through His resurrection, "by His death trampling upon death and bestowing life to those in the graves." The final stage in the grief process for the Christian is not the acceptance of death but its transformation into life eternal through the resurrection of our Lord Jesus. "But in fact Christ has been raised from the dead, the first fruits of those who have fallen asleep... For as in Adam all die, so also in Christ shall all be made alive" (1 Cor. 15:20,22).

I asked her how long it had been since her mother died, and she said a year.

I replied that my mother had died ten years before and I still grieved, though less often. I assured her that grieving was right. Then the student smiled and said she felt very relieved to hear it. I guess in this day of fast food, we try to have fast grief, but our human nature is too ancient and rooted to bear it.

~ A. Gardiner

The Valley of Dry Bones (Ezekiel 37)

"Can these bones live again?" is a question often asked at the grave of a loved one. "Yes" is the triumphant shout of Ezekiel's vision (Ezekiel 37). "If the Spirit of Him Who raised Jesus from the dead dwells in you, He Who raised Christ Jesus from the grave will give life to your mortal bodies through his Spirit Who dwells in you" (Rom. 8:11).

"Thus says the Lord God to these bones, 'Behold I will cause breath to enter you and will cause flesh to come upon you and cover you with skin and put breath in you, and you shall live and know that I am the Lord..." (Ezek. 37:5-6).

He did it for Lazarus who had been dead four days. He did it for the daughter of Jairus. He did it for the son of the widow of Nain. He did it for Jesus Who rose from the tomb after three days. He will do it at the end of time when the dead shall hear His voice and come forth from the graves. He does it for us today when we come to Him with our "dry bones", our dead hopes and broken dreams, and fills us with the faith and hope of life eternal.

Ezekiel's vision is no longer a vision. It was a vision in the Old Testament. In the New Testament it becomes a reality when the Resurrected Christ breathes His Spirit into our dry, grief-stricken bones as He will do on the Last Day.

What is sown is perishable,
What is raised is imperishable.
But thanks be to God, who gives us this
victory through our Lord Jesus Christ.

~ 1 Corinthians 15

ABOUT THE AUTHOR

Anthony M. Coniaris

Father Anthony M. Coniaris has served at St. Mary's Greek Orthodox Church in Minneapolis, Minnesota, since 1948. Ordained a Deacon in 1950 and a Priest in 1953, he is a native of Boston, Massachusetts, where he attended the Boston Latin School. He is a graduate of the Holy Cross Greek Orthodox Theological Seminary in Brookline, Massachusetts, as well as the Northwestern Theological Seminary in Minneapolis. He has attended postgraduate studies in the fields of religion and psychiatry at the University of Minnesota and at St. John's University in Collegeville, Minnesota.

Father Coniaris has been in charge of Eastern Orthodox student work at the University of Minnesota, where he served on the Council of Religious Advisors. He has served on the Standing Committee of Liturgical Translations of the Archdiocese. He was also an adjunct Professor of Homiletics at Holy Cross Seminary.

He is past President of the Minneapolis Ministerial Association, the Twin Cities Metropolitan Church Commission, the Minneapolis Professional Men's Club, the Minneapolis Kiwanis, and the Greater Minneapolis Council of Churches. He was a member of the Board of the Children's Heart Fund, and is listed in WHO'S WHO in RELIGION

1976-77. He received the WCCO Good Neighbor Award in 1973 and the Alumnus Citation from Holy Cross Seminary.

He retired in January 1993 after serving at St. Mary's for 44 years. He is currently the President of Light & Life Publishing Company. He is the author of over 85 books, pamphlets and brochures.

Available titles authored by Anthony M. Coniaris

Introducing the Orthodox Church
My Daily Orthodox Prayer Book
Making God Real in the Orthodox Christian Home
Let's Take A Walk Through Our Orthodox Church
Your Baby's Baptism in the Orthodox Church
Nicene Creed For Young People
Surviving the Loss of a Loved One
Confronting and Controlling Thoughts
Philokalia: The Bible of Orthodox Spirituality
A Beginner's Introduction to the Philokalia
Tools for Theosis
God & You: Person to Person
Discovering God
Christ's Comfort for Those Who Sorrow

Titles by Anthony M. Coniaris
available at www.light-n-life.com

Light & Life Retreats & Seminars©

Learn to Live the Orthodox Faith

Is your church looking for a retreat leader who can present ancient Orthodox truths in a practical and contemporary fashion without watering down the wisdom of our Church? Our Light & Life presenter, Daniel Christopulos, is available for retreats, seminars or lectures prepared from the following Light & Life publications authored by our beloved Fr. Anthony Coniaris. The three books below are topics for the currently offered Light & Life Retreats & Seminars©:

Tools for Theosis ~ Becoming God-like Through Christ

God and You: Person to Person

Making God Real in the Orthodox Christian Home

Fr. Anthony Coniaris is the Founder and President of Light & Life Publishing Company and has authored over eighty-five books and pamphlets. Presenter Daniel Christopulos has served many years in US Orthodox parishes, been an Orthodox missionary in Africa where he taught at the Archbishop Makarios III Seminary in Nairobi, Kenya, taught at the high school, college and university levels, and been a national trainer for the US Department of Health and Human Services Office of Adolescent Pregnancy Programs. He currently is the US Country Representative for International Orthodox Christian Charities (IOCC) where he has worked since 2001.

Retreats are tailored to your specific time frame in full-day (9am – 3pm) or a day-and-a-half format (typically Friday night and all day Saturday). Lectures, seminars and other longer retreats can also be designed to fit your parishes' spiritual needs.

For more details, please email patty@light-n-life.com or call 952-200-9566. We look forward to partnering with you in strengthening the spiritual life of your church.